Taxcafe.co.uk Tax Guides

# Tax Saving Tactics for Motorists

A Guide for Company Owners,
Sole Traders & Landlords

By Christopher Field FCCA

# Important Legal Notices

Taxcafe®
TAX GUIDE – "Tax Saving Tactics for Motorists"

**Published by:**
Taxcafe UK Limited
67 Milton Road
Kirkcaldy
KY1 1TL
United Kingdom
Tel: (01592) 560081

First Edition, September 2011

ISBN 978-1-907302-49-7

**Disclaimer**
Before reading or relying on the content of this Tax Guide, please read
carefully the disclaimer. If you have queries then please contact the
publisher at team@taxcafe.co.uk.

## Need Affordable & Expert Tax Planning Help?

### Try Taxcafe's Unique Question & Answer Service

The purpose of Taxcafe guides is to provide you with detailed guidance, giving you all the information you need to make informed decisions.

Ultimately, you may want to take further action or obtain guidance personal to your circumstances.

Taxcafe.co.uk has a unique online tax help service that provides access to highly qualified tax professionals at an affordable rate.

For more information or to take advantage of this service please visit:

## www.taxcafe.co.uk/questions

## BUSINESS TAX SAVER

If you like this tax guide...

You will also like *Business Tax Saver*...

Our monthly guide to BIG business tax savings

<u>You can try it now for FREE!</u>

Go to www.taxcafe.co.uk/businesstaxsaver.html

# Disclaimer

1. Please note that this publication is intended as **general guidance only** and does NOT constitute accountancy, tax, financial or other professional advice. The author and Taxcafe UK Limited make no representations or warranties with respect to the accuracy or completeness of the contents of this publication and cannot accept any responsibility for any liability, loss or risk, personal or otherwise, which may arise, directly or indirectly, from reliance on information contained in this publication.

2. Please note that tax legislation, the law and practices of government and regulatory authorities (e.g. HM Revenue & Customs) are constantly changing. Furthermore, your personal circumstances may vary from the general information contained in this tax guide which may not be suitable for your situation. We therefore recommend that for accountancy, tax, financial or other professional advice, you consult a suitably qualified accountant, tax specialist, independent financial adviser, or other professional adviser. Your professional adviser will be able to provide specific advice based on your personal circumstances.

3. Please note that Taxcafe UK Limited has relied wholly on the expertise of the author in the preparation of the content of this publication. The author is not an employee of Taxcafe UK Limited but has been selected by Taxcafe UK Limited using reasonable care and skill to write the content of this publication.

4. All persons described in the examples in this guide are entirely fictional characters. Any similarities to actual persons, living or dead are entirely coincidental.

# About the Author

Christopher Field is a Chartered Certified Accountant living in Purley Oaks, Surrey. He qualified in 1988 and spent the early part of his career in financial services before setting up on his own with Acumen Accounting in 2000. He specialises in tax planning and compliance work for small companies and has built a strong local reputation.

When he is not helping his clients with their accounts and tax returns, Chris enjoys writing articles, inventing computer games, busying himself around the house and spending time with his friends and family. His future plans include writing more books, expanding his company and touring the world with his wife, Svetlana.

## Dedication

To Svetlana, for all your love and support.

# Contents

# Contents

# Contents

# Contents

# Contents

# Introduction

One of the most common questions we get asked by business owners is: "How do I save tax on my car?" It's right up there with: "How much should I pay my spouse?" or "How much profit have I made this year?"

Like many tax questions, the honest answer is: "It depends", which is why we decided to write a whole guide on the subject.

A car is more than just a business asset. For many people it's their pride and joy. You don't choose a car for business reasons alone, you choose it for personal reasons too. You might decide to buy a particular model because you like the style or quality or because it has a certain kind of kudos or panache.

You might go for the comfort of an executive saloon, the high performance of a sports car or the 'je ne sais quoi' of a classic model! On the other hand, you might eschew all those things and simply go for reliability, functionality and value for money. You might be environmentally conscious and insist on a car with low $CO_2$ emissions or maybe you just like the colour!

The point is, we all have our own preferences when it comes to choosing a car and they reflect our own tastes and personality more than any other possession, apart from perhaps our clothes.

The taxman recognises this too and as a result there are special tax rules for cars. You don't get taxed more for working in a swanky office or for having a state of the art computer. Cars, on the other hand, are regarded as personal possessions as well as business assets.

Company cars, in particular, tend to be quite heavily taxed, depending on their value and environmental credentials. Needless to say, the most expensive cars are usually the most desirable and hence the most highly taxed, although there are now some quite attractive 'green' cars on the market.

This guide will show you how to save tax on your business motoring and make key decisions, for example whether to get your company to buy a car or keep it in your own name. We will look at the tax rules relating to vans and pool cars, the various VAT

1

aspects and other tax issues related to motoring, such as workplace parking and penalty notices.

Throughout the book you will find many handy tables and case studies that will help you make the best choice.

In order to save tax on your motoring you first have to understand the basics. Part 1 of this book therefore explains the various tax rules affecting business motorists.

Part 2 explains how to save tax on your business motoring. This is achieved by identifying and analysing 10 key decisions you may have to make. Case studies and tables are used to illustrate how various factors impact on these decisions.

Hopefully, after reading this book, you will better understand the sometimes complex relationship between cars and taxes.

More importantly, however, you will learn to recognise and take advantage of any tax-planning opportunities that may present themselves and thus save tax on your car.

## Landlords and Property Investors

Throughout this guide we refer to 'sole traders'. This term applies equally to most landlords and property investors. HM Revenue and Customs treats these individuals as self-employed business owners hence many of the tax saving strategies apply equally to landlords and other property business owners.

One exception is in the area of reclaiming VAT. Most landlords are not VAT registered and therefore cannot reclaim VAT on any of their motoring costs. Similarly most landlords do not have to pay national insurance on their rental profits.

Some landlords use a company to invest in property and can therefore get their companies to buy a car for their private use. Hence the chapters on company cars apply equally to landlords with property companies.

# Part 1

# How Cars Are Taxed

# Chapter 1

## Company Cars

### A Bit of History

Probably the most familiar aspect of business motoring is the company car. They've been around for a long time now and are almost as old as the internal combustion engine itself.

However, it was not until the 1960s that company cars became commonplace. The construction of the motorways and a general improvement in the UK's road network made it much easier for sales staff to visit their suppliers and customers and this fuelled a rapid increase in business travel.

A vast army of travelling salesmen were given company cars to drive all over the country, promoting their firms' products and acting as the face of the business. This was an important role in the days before the internet and improved telecommunications made trading and customer service less labour intensive, albeit more remote and impersonal.

At that time cars were normally only given to those employees who actually needed them as a tool of the job, much the same as laptop computers are today. During the 1970s, however, cars came to be seen as a perk for senior executives and there were several reasons for this development.

Firstly, it was a time of mandatory wage restraint. The governments of the day tried to impose strict limits on increases in both incomes and prices in a futile attempt to control inflation, and businesses found it hard to retain key personnel by giving them pay rises. Benefits such as company cars were an attractive alternative that were not subject to Government interference.

Tax was also a driver. Income tax for high earners rose to astronomical levels in the 1970s (tax rates were as high as 83% at one point) and the benefit-in-kind regime was tame by comparison.

The rampant inflation of the 1970s and 1980s was the other main factor – incredibly cars were depreciating in value more slowly than the money needed to buy them. Soon, company cars came to be seen as an essential part of the executive remuneration package, with their connotations of image, rank and status.

Inevitably the taxman caught up with all this and a special tax regime for company cars was introduced in 1976. In those days the tax was based on a set of scale rates related to engine size and it was considered appropriate to maintain a distinction between cars that were workhorses and those that were essentially perks, with little or no business use. Those driving a large number of miles in the normal course of their work paid less tax than those who only used their company car to visit their chums at the golf club.

Of course, none of this did the environment much good. All of those company cars pumped more and more exhaust fumes into the atmosphere, wore out the roads and added to congestion. So when the world woke up to climate change in the 1990s, it was decided that the whole system of company car taxation needed to be reformed.

The current tax system is based on $CO_2$ emissions. Company car users are rewarded for 'going green', those who drive gas guzzlers pay through the nose. No allowance is made for business mileage, so it no longer matters how many miles you drive.

The new regime was designed to be fiscally neutral (meaning that the overall amount of tax raised was to be the same) and to some extent this was true as the maximum taxable benefit remained at 35% of the car's list price. However, the general perception among company car users is that they are worse off under the current tax regime.

Cars with relatively high $CO_2$ emissions are taxed more severely now than when the current tax regime was first introduced but the cap is still set at 35% of list price, so the worst offenders are not actually suffering much more than they did originally.

As expected, the motor industry responded by producing cars with much lower $CO_2$ emissions. Today there are far fewer company cars on the road than in 2000 and they are much cleaner than they were 10 years ago. According to an Inland Revenue report, removing the link between tax and mileage alone resulted in company car users driving up to 400 million less business miles per year than under the old tax regime.

Why have numbers of company cars fallen so much? It could be because the reforms have made the tax burden on company cars much more visible and topical than it was before and made people realise just how much their status symbol was costing. Other reasons include the greater willingness of employers to offer cash alternatives, the growing popularity of employee car ownership schemes and less need for sales staff to have company cars (and indeed less need for the sales staff themselves) with the growth of the internet and e-commerce over the last 10-15 years.

However, the company car is a sturdy beast, and there is recent evidence that it is making a comeback. This is probably spurred on by the fact that most manufacturers now offer some very attractive models in the 'green' market and more people are willing to accept an environmentally-friendly vehicle. There are also some attractive salary sacrifice schemes on offer now that make company cars much more tax-efficient than they used to be.

## What is a Company Car?

Before looking at the tax calculations in more detail, it is important to explain what we mean by the term 'company car'. Firstly, what is a car? The taxman has an official definition: a car is any mechanically propelled road vehicle but excludes:

- Goods vehicles (e.g. lorries)
- Motorcycles
- Invalid carriages (for people with physical disabilities)
- Vehicles unsuitable for private use, e.g. Grand Prix cars

HMRC also has a definition of a van, but we will look at this later in Chapter 5.

A company car is a car that is made available to an employee (or any member of their family or household) *by reason of their employment* for their *personal use*.

That last point is very important. A car is only a taxable benefit if it is available for personal use. Unfortunately the term 'available for personal use' is interpreted very widely when it comes to company cars. Once you have been given custody of the keys on an ongoing basis it is extremely difficult to prove that there was no personal use, even if your employer has specifically prohibited it.

Taking a car home with you and parking it overnight in your own neighbourhood is evidence of personal use. That is because home-to-work commuting nearly always counts as personal use. Note that the car merely has to be *made available* to you for personal use. It is irrelevant whether or not you actually do make personal use of the vehicle – or drive it at all for that matter.

This makes it vital for employers to strictly control the use of cars that are used mainly as workhorses for the business if they are not to land their employees with unnecessary tax bills. If a car is used essentially as a tool of the trade, it is important to ensure that no private use is either permitted or possible. All employees with access to the car must be told that no private use is allowed, even during the course of company business, and the keys should only be issued when the car is needed for work purposes. This will mean keeping good records, such as mileage logs, and making sure that no one has access to the keys without permission.

A taxable company car benefit can sometimes arise entirely unexpectedly. It is not just salesmen and executives who are taxed on them; anyone might be if they regularly use a company vehicle for any reason whatsoever. The rules are much stricter than people think.

## Taxable Persons

### *Higher Paid Employees*

Only directors and 'higher paid' employees have to pay tax on their company cars. Unfortunately, 'higher paid' employees are extremely common these days because the amount of income you have to earn for the taxman to treat you as higher paid has been frozen at £8,500 since 1979!

Bear in mind that the £8,500 threshold includes the value of the car benefit itself and any motoring expenses incurred by the employee in connection with the vehicle, such as fuel or garage bills paid with a company credit card or reimbursed on an expense claim.

This exemption has now withered on the vine so much that very few people benefit from it. Nevertheless there may still be a few part-time workers with company cars who remain exempt.

## Directors

When we talk about directors we must include members of their family or household. I've lost count of the number of questions I've seen on tax forums from directors asking if they can avoid tax by simply giving a car to their spouse or, more sneakily, by giving them a "sales job" and a luxury car to do it with.

The taxman would look askance at any such arrangement. He would ask whether any other employees in the company receive similar cars for doing the same kind of work. He would also question whether it is normal commercial practice for staff in that sector to be given luxury cars. Even if the car is not a luxury model and other staff get them too, the taxman is very likely to ask what sort of work your spouse does, how much time is spent doing it and why the car is needed at all.

The same also goes for other relatives, unmarried partners, and friends. If a director is seen as passing on a benefit to someone else that really belongs to the director, the director will be taxed on it.

## Shadow Directors

You can't even get away with choosing *not* to be a director. If you are what the taxman calls a 'shadow director' you will be treated for tax purposes as though you are a real director. A shadow director is a person on whose instructions or recommendations the board of directors of a company are accustomed to act.

This label normally applies to majority shareholders who wish to avoid disclosure as a director, but it can apply to you even if you hold no shares in a company at all. For example, in a 2001 Court of Appeal decision, a shadow director was found to be someone who exerts real influence over a company's affairs, so the net is cast fairly widely on this one.

### Non-Employees

It should also be noted that a car benefit can arise on anyone who is a worker. This term is not necessarily restricted to employees. In most areas of legislation it includes other individuals too, including most agency workers, some freelancers and short-term casual workers.

Only the self-employed are excluded from the definition of employee for tax purposes. It is most unlikely that anyone who is not an employee would get a company car anyway, but in theory they could, and in that case you would have to report a car benefit. You wouldn't be able to avoid tax simply by hiring someone through an agency, for example.

### Family Members

There is one sensible exemption that the self-employed may wish to note. Where an employer is an individual (i.e. a sole trader as opposed to a company) and provides an employee with a car in the normal course of a family or personal relationship, such as a father buying a car for his son who also happens to be his employee, then this can be ignored for tax purposes.

However, the employer has to ensure that the car is not treated as a business asset and that none of the running costs are paid by the business or claimed against tax.

Notwithstanding this, there is nothing to stop such a car being used for business journeys. It is also permissible in such cases for the employee to be reimbursed for business mileage at the approved tax-free mileage rates (45p for the first 10,000 miles; 25p thereafter).

This is quite a common situation in most family businesses, and the important point here is to pay the employee mileage rather than simply reimburse their fuel or other motoring costs (apart from parking or road tolls which are allowed in addition).

# Exemptions from Company Car Tax

## *Disabled Drivers*

Disabled drivers do not receive a blanket exemption but can be exempt if their employer provides a car specifically for home-to-work travel. The car must have been adapted for the disabled employee's special needs (or can be an automatic if the employee's disability prevents them from driving a car with manual transmission).

To be tax exempt the car must also be available only for commuting to and from work or for getting to and from training courses allowable as a trading expense for the employer. No other travel must be permitted by the employer and no other travel must in fact be made by the disabled person in that car.

It is not clear how these rules are meant to be enforced. Presumably the employer is supposed to check the expected mileage against the odometer at the end of each tax year, but it is hard to imagine someone using a car just to get to work and not doing the weekend shopping in it too.

If a disabled employee does get caught for company car tax, there is another concession that may help to reduce it. When calculating the taxable benefit in kind, if the employee can only drive automatic cars due to his/her disability, both the list price and the $CO_2$ emissions can be reduced to that of the nearest manual equivalent where this is lower (as it usually is). However, the employee must be a blue badge holder in order to qualify for this relief.

## *No Private Use*

A car may also be exempt when an employer specifically prohibits private use and no such private use has in fact taken place, even though technically the car may have been available for private use. Usually this would only be relevant for cars which are parked overnight at or near the workplace but do not qualify as pool cars for some reason, perhaps because one employee uses it more or less exclusively. It would be necessary for the employer to keep a detailed mileage log and have safe custody of the keys between journeys in order to satisfy this exemption and certainly to prevent employees taking the car home.

It is theoretically possible for an employee working from home to keep the car there and still satisfy the exemption. Obviously there would be no question of the car being used for commuting if the employee only ever worked from home.

The main issue would be proving that there was no private use. Firstly, the employer would need to expressly prohibit private use, a condition which could be easily satisfied by making it part of the employment contract. Secondly, it would be necessary for the employee to keep a very detailed mileage log reconciled to the odometer at the end of each tax year, with no gaps or variances.

In reality, the taxman would purse his lips at such an arrangement. It is not unknown for tax inspectors to check the fuel bills and query them if the car was regularly filled up near the home of the employee, or at a supermarket where it could have been used for shopping too. However, it would be easy to refute this if the fuel was bought on the same day as a business trip, and as for supermarkets they seem to own most of the petrol stations now anyway. It would also greatly assist your case if you or your partner already had a vehicle for your own personal use and it was not necessary to use the company one.

### Emergency Vehicles

Drivers of emergency vehicles are also entitled to an exemption from company car tax if they take their vehicles home at night. The driver must work for an emergency service (e.g., police, fire, ambulance).

An emergency vehicle is defined as a vehicle that is designed to respond to emergencies and has a fixed flashing light. Fixed means it must be a permanent fitting.

There is an exclusion from the fixed flashing light rule where such a light could endanger the security of the emergency service worker, for example if the car is used by a police officer in danger of being targeted by terrorists or other criminals.

There is one further condition – the emergency vehicle must be provided on terms which prohibit its personal use other than when the driver is on call to respond to emergencies or is engaged in on-call commuting, and the driver must only use it in those circumstances.

Of course, it is mainly the police that benefit from this exemption (it is hard to imagine a fire engine or ambulance being parked outside someone's home overnight).

## *Test and Demonstration Cars*

The only other exemption from the company car tax rules is for employees in the motor industry who are in charge of demonstration, test and experimental vehicles. Where, as part of their normal duties, sales staff or demonstrators have to take such a vehicle home for the express purpose of calling on a potential customer the next day, the vehicle will not on that account alone be regarded as available for private use.

However, this exemption will not be granted if the vehicle is otherwise available for private use, such as at weekends (unless the employee happens to be seeing a potential customer with the vehicle over the weekend) or when the employee is on holiday.

The same goes for employees who are in charge of test cars for experimental or development purposes. The taxman concedes that, in certain types of test such as cold-starting, it is not possible to conduct the tests properly without the cars being available for private use. Therefore, no car benefit will arise in these circumstances provided that the primary use of the car is testing and any private use is incidental to this.

This exemption does not apply if private use becomes the main purpose, such as when the car is taken on holiday.

# Chapter 2

# Company Car Tax

## Steps in the Calculation

Tax on company cars is based mainly on 2 things:

- Manufacturer's list price, and
- $CO_2$ emissions.

The table below shows the taxable percentages applicable to the 2011/12, 2012/13 and 2013/14 tax years.

You will note that the rates are going up at each $CO_2$ level, as they have done since the new system was introduced in 2002, apart from the very highest emissions which remain capped at 35%. The increases reflect the fact that cars are getting 'greener' each year as manufacturers strive to reduce $CO_2$ levels.

So how much tax do you pay on a company car?

Let's say you are a higher-rate taxpayer and your company car runs on petrol, has $CO_2$ emissions of 143 g/km and a list price of £15,000. For the current 2011/12 tax year the appropriate percentage is 18% (see table). This means you will have a taxable benefit-in-kind of £2,700 and an income tax bill of £1,080:

£15,000 x 18% x 40% income tax = £1,080

The taxable percentage will increase to 19% in 2012/13 and 20% in 2013/14, resulting in income tax bills of £1,140 and £1,200 respectively.

There is no employee's national insurance on the taxable benefit but the company will pay employer's national insurance at 13.8%.

So for the current 2011/12 tax year the employer's national insurance bill will be:

£15,000 x 18% x 13.8% = £373

# Company Cars
## Taxable % of List Price

| CO$_2$ g/km | | | |
|---|---|---|---|
| **2011/12** | **2012/13** | **2013/14** | **Appropriate %** |
| 0 | 0 | 0 | Exempt |
| 1-75 | 1-75 | 1-75 | 5% |
| 76-120 | 76-99 | 76-94 | 10% |
| - | 100-104 | 95-99 | 11% |
| - | 105-109 | 100-104 | 12% |
| - | 110-114 | 105-109 | 13% |
| - | 115-119 | 110-114 | 14% |
| 121-129 | 120-125 | 115-119 | 15% |
| 130-134 | 125-129 | 120-124 | 16% |
| 135-139 | 130-134 | 125-129 | 17% |
| 140-144 | 135-139 | 130-134 | 18% |
| 145-149 | 140-144 | 135-139 | 19% |
| 150-154 | 145-149 | 140-144 | 20% |
| 155-159 | 150-154 | 145-149 | 21% |
| 160-164 | 155-159 | 150-154 | 22% |
| 165-169 | 160-164 | 155-159 | 23% |
| 170-174 | 165-169 | 160-164 | 24% |
| 175-179 | 170-174 | 165-169 | 25% |
| 180-184 | 175-179 | 170-174 | 26% |
| 185-189 | 180-184 | 175-179 | 27% |
| 190-194 | 185-189 | 180-184 | 28% |
| 195-199 | 190-194 | 185-189 | 29% |
| 200-204 | 195-199 | 190-194 | 30% |
| 205-209 | 200-204 | 195-199 | 31% |
| 210-214 | 205-209 | 200-204 | 32% |
| 215-219 | 210-214 | 205-209 | 33% |
| 220-224 | 215-219 | 210-214 | 34% |
| 225 or more | 220 or more | 215 or more | 35% |

**Notes:**
1. Add an extra 3% for diesels, subject to a maximum of 35%
2. Cars and vans with zero $CO_2$ emissions are exempt from company car tax for a 5-year period starting in 2010-11

Calculating your company car tax may be a little bit more involved than in the above simple illustration.

The full number of steps is as follows:

1) Find the manufacturer's list price

2) Add accessories not included in the list price

3) Deduct any capital contributions made by the employee (up to a maximum of £5,000)

4) Find the $CO_2$ emissions figure

5) Look up the appropriate percentage for that emissions figure (add 3% for diesels)

6) Multiply the adjusted list price by the appropriate percentage

7) Adjust the taxable benefit for any qualifying periods of unavailability (see Step 7 below)

8) Deduct any contributions by the employee towards private use of the car (apart from fuel or specific costs)

9) The income tax payable will be the car benefit multiplied by the employee's top rate of tax (20%, 40% or 50%)

Employees pay income tax (but not national insurance) on the taxable car benefit. Employers pay Class 1A national insurance at 13.8% on the benefit.

We will now look at each of the above steps in detail.

### Step 1 - List Price

The list price is the price published by the manufacturer, importer or distributor on the day before the car was first registered. Finding the list price is usually just a matter of checking with the manufacturer or main dealer. If not, there are some handy websites where you will find it, for example www.comcar.co.uk

You need to be very careful to look up the exact model, as most makes of car have a very wide range and they all tend to vary in price. You must also include VAT, any customs or excise duty, delivery costs and number plates to obtain the total price on which tax is calculated.

It is important to note that the original list price must be used even if you buy the car second hand. You cannot use the purchase price instead.

I've had to disappoint many a client down the years who thought that selling his car to his company for a low price would be a good way of reducing company car tax.

Even those who buy new can make the mistake of using the dealer's advertised price. This is irrelevant as it will usually be less than the original list price.

### *Step 2 - Accessories*

Accessories are often overlooked but must be added to the taxable value of a company car. These are listed on the invoice if you buy the car new but are less easy to identify if you buy second hand. The only way to find out is to check with the manufacturer or dealer which fittings come as standard and look up the list price of any others. They will commonly include things like air conditioning, alloy wheels and in-car entertainment. Any such items must be added to the list price of the car.

You do not have to include accessories that belong to the employee, although the employee may be taxed on them separately if they were bought from the employer for less than their market value or given free of charge. The employee is also not taxed on loose items such as rugs, tools and maps.

Any equipment that you need to do your job is not taxed as an accessory. This will always include mobile phones whether you need them or not as they are specifically exempted from tax by the legislation.

The tax treatment of satnavs is less clear. If your job involves travelling to new destinations all the time, such as a sales rep visiting potential customers, then it would probably qualify as exempt equipment needed for your job. However, if you are an account manager visiting the same clients on a regular basis, then it would be hard to argue that it is a necessary tool of the job. In most cases you would probably get away with it though.

If the accessories were supplied with the car at the time it was purchased, you must always use the manufacturer's list price for them. If no list price is available, use a notional price based on current market value. The list price must be the one published on the day before the car was first registered. This rule applies even if you didn't buy the car until years later.

If the accessory was added after the car was first made available, you are allowed to use the list price as at the date it was added.

You can also ignore any items with a list price below £100. However, you are not allowed to split items up for that purpose. For example, if you add a set of alloy wheels costing £300 they cannot be valued at £75 each.

When a replacement accessory is of the same kind and not superior to the old accessory, then you ignore it completely and just continue using the price of the old accessory. Otherwise, you must add the list price of the replacement accessory.

You are normally allowed to deduct the list price of the old accessory, but not if it was a standard accessory that was included in the list price of the car, so effectively you could end up being taxed twice on the same item if it was a standard fitting.

It is worth noting that some accessories such as air conditioning may affect the $CO_2$ emissions of the car. This will be reflected in the emissions figure shown on the registration document if it is a standard fitting. Some lighter alloy wheels actually reduce a car's $CO_2$ emissions. However, if accessories are not standard fittings, they cannot reduce the official $CO_2$ emissions figure as this is fixed once and for all.

### Step 3 - Capital Contributions

Any capital contributions made by an employee towards the cost of the car reduce the taxable benefit. This often happens when an employee wants a more expensive car than he would otherwise be entitled to and offers to pay the difference. However, there is a £5,000 limit. If the employee contributes more than this, the balance is disregarded.

Capital contributions must be distinguished from payments for private use which are allowed separately. It is best to put them in writing and obtain the money from the employee before the car is made available.

Capital contributions are disregarded if they are subsequently paid back to the employee, either directly or indirectly, for example in the form of a pay rise or some other benefit.

However, employers are allowed to rebate part of the capital contribution if the car is subsequently sold.

### Step 4 - CO₂ Emissions

With very few exceptions, all cars are now taxed on their carbon dioxide emissions. The $CO_2$ figure is set for the life of the car. It is the one shown on the certificate summarising the results of the type approval test when the car is first registered. This does not change even if its actual $CO_2$ emissions increase over time.

The taxable percentages are shown in the table above and the relevant $CO_2$ emissions figure can be found on the V5 Registration Document for vehicles registered on or after 1 March 2001. If the car was registered before then (but after 31 December 1997) you can obtain the $CO_2$ emissions figure from the Vehicle Certification Agency. Their website is http://carfueldata.direct.gov.uk

Unfortunately this website is not much help for older cars as it only shows the latest $CO_2$ figures for new cars currently on sale in the UK. However, you may be able to find historic data in a downloaded or printed version of a VCA booklet called "New Car Fuel Consumption and Emissions Figures" that was current at the time. The website will be useful if you cannot find the V5 document for a car registered fairly recently.

If a car registered on or after 1 January 1998 does not have an approved $CO_2$ emissions figure, it will be necessary to go by the cylinder capacity to determine the taxable value.

These are as follows:

**Cylinder capacity (cubic centimetres)    Taxable %**

| 1,400 or less | 15% |
| More than 1,400 but not more than 2,000 | 25% |
| More than 2,000 | 35% |

This is assuming that the car has an internal combustion engine and one or more reciprocating pistons. There are some that don't, for example electric cars powered by a battery or a car with a rotary Wankel engine.

Any other cars not fitting the above description have a taxable value of 35% of list price (or the notional price if no list price was ever published).

Cars registered before 1 January 1998 are also taxed on their cylinder capacity, even if they happen to have an approved $CO_2$ emissions figure. The relevant percentages are as follows:

**Cylinder capacity (cubic centimetres)    Taxable %**

| 1,400 or less | 15% |
| More than 1,400 but not more than 2,000 | 22% |
| More than 2,000 | 32% |

So any high mileage salesmen upset by the new tax rules in 2002 can continue to get 15% on their cars if they still have them and they fulfil the above criteria. Of course, any such vehicle still in existence would have enough miles on the clock by now to have travelled to the moon!

### Step 5 – The Appropriate Percentage

The percentages applicable to various $CO_2$ levels are updated each year and can be found on the HMRC website and those of motoring organisations such as the AA and RAC. Simply read off the percentage for the relevant $CO_2$ band, but remember to add 3% for diesels.

## Step 6 – The Taxable Value

Now multiply the List Price by the Appropriate Percentage to find the taxable value of the car. This is always rounded down to the nearest pound and represents the base value which will appear on your annual P11D unless there are any further adjustments.

## Step 7 - Periods of Unavailability

Sometimes a company car benefit may only arise for part of the year, for example when someone joins or leaves a company or receives a promotion entitling them to a company car.

Sometimes it could be because the car is unavailable for some reason. A classic example of this came when I was working for a merchant bank back in the 1980s. One of my tasks was to compile the company car data for the annual P11Ds, and a guy called Vince knocked on my door and said that he ought to get a reduction in his tax bill. "Why's that?" I asked him. "Because I took it onto a beach in Somerset last week and it got stuck in the sand. Then the tide came in and submerged it."

Vince was lucky because it took quite a while to dig the car out and get it to a garage for repairs, and inevitably it was a write-off. He therefore got his tax deduction. Anything less than 30 days and the period of unavailability must be ignored, unless the car turns out to be *permanently* unavailable, which of course it was in this highly unusual case.

In fact, Vince got a permanent reduction in his tax bill because the bank wouldn't let him have another car after that and a memo went around the building warning all company car users not to drive their vehicles on to beaches or swamps. So it was pretty embarrassing for him too!

There wasn't much doubt about the unavailability of the car in that particular case but sometimes it's not so clear-cut.

It is always the car that must be unavailable to the employee, not the other way round. You cannot obtain a reduction in your company car tax because you are physically absent, for example on holiday or a business trip, or because you are ill or injured.

The same goes for people who are disqualified from driving or no longer have a valid license.

Likewise, a car does not become unavailable simply because the insurance, tax or MOT has expired, or because it has run out of petrol or the tyres have gone flat. It must be physically incapable of being driven for at least 30 days, unless it has been permanently withdrawn. This normally means that it must be in a garage or other place where it is undergoing repairs and cannot be driven away by the user in the meantime.

The car must be physically withdrawn from the user in order for it to be unavailable, and this normally means handing the keys to someone who cannot be ordered by you to give them back again. Otherwise bosses could avoid the tax simply by giving the keys to their staff.

If your company car is unavailable for less than 30 days you are still taxed on it even if you are not given a replacement car to drive in the meantime. Replacement cars are generally ignored for the first 30 days. If, however, your normal car is unavailable for 30 days or more and you receive a replacement car, then your tax for that period will be based on the replacement car.

How much is the tax reduced by if a car is unavailable? You simply reduce the taxable benefit proportionally. P11D software packages will do this for you if you enter the relevant dates. There are also free calculators on the HMRC website.

### *Step 8 - Contributions for Private Use*

Employers often require their staff to make personal contributions towards the private use of their company cars. Normally such contributions are allowable as a deduction against the car benefit.

However, there are a few traps for the unwary.

Firstly, the employee must actually be *required* to pay contributions for private use of the car. The deduction is not allowed if the employee pays them voluntarily. The contributions must also be actually paid and not made as part of some loan arrangement. A deduction from the employee's salary is ideal.

22

Secondly, the contributions must not actually be for some other purpose, such as getting a better car than the employee would otherwise have been entitled to. This is quite a common arrangement if the car is leased and employers must make sure that up-grade payments are not mixed up with other contributions for private use.

As with capital contributions, there must be no arrangement whereby the employee gets the money back later or receives a pay rise or some other benefit in lieu of their personal use contributions.

It is possible to restrict personal use contributions to certain groups of employees, provided the rules are impartial.

It is important to ensure that personal use contributions are kept completely separate from the running costs of the car. For example, if the employer requires the user to pay for insurance or maintenance, this will not qualify as a personal use contribution. Such costs must be paid directly by the employer, reimbursed to the employee or borne by the employee as a completely separate arrangement to the personal use charges.

Personal use contributions must also be kept separate from fuel payments for private mileage or personal contributions towards a fuel benefit. However, it is allowed for the employer to charge for personal use on a mileage basis, so that those employees who have the most private use pay more.

### Step 9 – Calculating the Tax

How much income tax do you actually have to pay on your company car benefit? A basic-rate taxpayer (generally speaking someone who earns less than £42,475 in the current 2011/12 tax year) will pay 20%, a higher-rate taxpayer will pay 40% and if you are one of those lucky people who earn more than £150,000 you will fall into the additional rate bracket and pay 50%!

There is better news concerning national insurance, at least for employees. No national insurance is payable on car or fuel benefit by employees as benefits-in-kind are not subject to Class 1 national insurance. However, employers are liable to Class IA national insurance on all benefits-in-kind (other than those that are specifically exempt) at a flat rate of 13.8% without any upper limit.

The fact that benefits are exempt from employee national insurance should be taken into account when assessing the value of cash alternatives offered by employers in place of company cars.

## Special Rules

### *Older Cars*

Sometimes the list price is not published on older cars and then you have to use its 'notional price'. This is the price which might reasonably have been expected to have been the list price at the time the car was first registered. We are talking about very old cars here as manufacturers have been obliged to publish list prices since 2001.

Obviously there is scope for different valuations and you would need to do as much research as possible to show that the one you used was reasonable. Older cars obviously have lower list prices than their modern day counterparts due to inflation. No adjustment is required for this, so in effect you do still get a tax discount for older cars.

### *Diesel Cars*

By far the most common adjustment is for diesel cars. You must always add 3% to the appropriate percentage for diesels. The reason for the 3% adjustment is that diesels emit other gases harmful to the environment, even though their $CO_2$ emissions tend to be lower. However, diesels cannot be taxed at more than 35% of list price, so if the appropriate percentage is 33% or more the increase will be restricted accordingly.

### *Road Fuel Gas*

There is a concession for cars manufactured to run on road fuel gas. The two most common types are compressed natural gas (CNG) and liquid petroleum gas (LPG).

If the car was either registered before the year 2000 or does not have an approved $CO_2$ emissions figure for both gas and another fuel, the extra cost of making the car capable of running on gas is deductible from the list price, so in effect you would only use the list price of an equivalent car that runs on petrol.

## Classic Cars

The rules are different for classic cars. A classic car is defined as follows:

- It must be at least 15 years old as at the end of the tax year
- It must have a market value of £15,000 or more, and
- The market value must exceed the list price or notional price of the car, plus accessories and less capital contributions

If all these conditions are satisfied, you must use the market value of the car that year instead of the list price or notional price.

This means that classic cars may actually cost you more tax because the original list price is usually much lower. Not many cars built 15 years ago are worth more than £15,000 today, so you can assume from this that a classic car must have some genuine investment value.

## The Old Price Cap

The old £80,000 cap on the list price for tax purposes was scrapped on 6th April 2011. You now have to use the actual list price for super-luxury cars.

In theory it is possible for an employee to be taxed more than he actually earns on a company car. Say for instance MI5 employs a special agent on a salary of £35,000 and gives him a £260,000 Lamborghini (including customised accessories such as ejector seats and rocket propelled grenades). The benefit in kind would be £91,000 and 40% tax would come to £36,400 which is more than the poor chap earns! It is not clear what is meant to happen in this situation.

The disappearance of the price cap could increase tax bills substantially for company directors with super-luxury cars who had previously calculated that they would be better off with a company car than taking an extra bonus or dividend to buy the car personally.

Anyone in this situation would be well advised to do the sums again and consider buying the car from the company if this saves money.

### *Shared Cars*

Sometimes company cars are shared by two or more employees over the course of a tax year. When this happens it is necessary to split the car benefit between them. There is no set formula for this split; any apportionment is acceptable so long as it is just and reasonable. However, the total car benefit of all employees must add up to the same as it would have been had the car been made available to just one employee.

The most common method of apportioning the taxable benefit of shared cars is by time spent. The employer would have to log exactly when the car was made available to each employee for private use.

In practice, the taxman would normally be unconcerned about the method of apportionment so long as the total is correct. However, he might take a closer look at any method which apportioned more benefit to basic-rate taxpayers than higher-rate taxpayers, especially if they happen to be married or related.

To qualify as a shared car, it must be made available for the private use of more than one employee **simultaneously**. For example, if there is a rota for private use and each employee has exclusive use of the car at a particular time, the periods of **exclusive** use must be disregarded in the apportionment as these must be assessed on each employee individually.

In certain circumstances it is quite possible for an employee to be taxed on the full car benefit even though other individuals use the car too.

## *Multiple Cars*

It is common in the motor industry for employees to drive a number of cars in the course of their work. Most of the time, these cars will be available for their private use too and are therefore taxable. An employee may have a number of cars available for private use at any one time, or may simply drive a different car every week or even every day.

Clearly the statutory rules are inappropriate in this situation, and the taxman therefore allows qualifying employers to use an averaging system. Qualifying employers include motor manufacturers, new car dealerships, used car traders, car leasing businesses, daily rental businesses and fleet operators.

Unfortunately this averaging system can get very complicated and it is best suited to large organisations with huge numbers of vehicles and employees who change cars frequently, where using the statutory rules would be even more onerous than the averaging method. To use this system, it is vital to keep detailed records of which vehicles are available at each location in your organisation and who is allowed to drive them.

# Fuel Benefit

In addition to tax on the car itself, an employee may also be taxed on the private fuel for that car, if the cost is incurred by the employer or a third party.

For the current 2011/12 tax year the tax is based on a fixed charge of £18,800. This amount is multiplied by the company car $CO_2$ emissions percentage, so the maximum charge is £6,580:

$$£18,800 \times 35\% = £6,580$$

A higher-rate taxpayer will then face a maximum income tax bill of £2,632:

$$£6,580 \times 40\% = £2,632$$

The employer will also face a maximum national insurance bill of £908 (£6,580 x 13.8%).

It does not matter how much private fuel is paid for by the employer, the fixed charge will apply in all cases. It also doesn't matter whether the employer pays for the fuel directly, for example on a corporate credit card, or reimburses the employee on expenses later.

The fuel benefit charge will apply even when the fuel was not specifically provided for private use. If the car itself is taxable then so is any fuel put into it by the employer.

Fuel used solely for business mileage is not taxable, but this will be difficult to prove if the car itself is available for private use. If the employer pays for any fuel at all, then it would be best to keep both a detailed mileage log and an analysis of all fuel costs borne by the employer showing dates, registration number, quantities and amounts. If fuel is ever siphoned out of one car and put into another, then obviously this should be noted too. If the costs and quantities are commensurate with the business mileage, this should be sufficient to prove that none of the fuel was available for private use.

An employee can avoid the fuel benefit charge by reimbursing the employer for any fuel relating to private use using mileage records and the latest advisory fuel rates. The latter are published by HM Revenue & Customs at least twice a year and can be found on their website at:

www.hmrc.gov.uk/cars/advisory_fuel_current.htm

For example, the advisory fuel rate for a 1600cc diesel car was 12p per litre in June 2011.

They may be called advisory but these fuel rates are more or less compulsory for company car users. It is very important to get this calculation right because, in theory at least, if an employer pays for just one drop of private fuel the employee will be clobbered for the whole £18,800 fuel benefit charge.

**The best course of action is usually to have the employee pay for ALL fuel and then claim for business mileage at the advisory rate.**

That way any mistakes can be made good later. Alternatively the employer can pay for all fuel and re-charge the employee for private use at the advisory rate. However, this method is more likely to lead to a tax charge as private mileage may not be reimbursed until after the end of the tax year. The employee must actually pay for all private use by the end of the tax year (or be required to do so as soon as possible afterwards) in order to avoid a fuel benefit tax charge.

It is very important not to mix up the advisory fuel rates with the approved tax free mileage rates for employees who *use their own* cars (currently 45p per mile for the first 10,000 miles and 25p thereafter). These rates are higher because they are meant to cover all the employee's costs, including depreciation.

In summary it is better for the employee to pay for all fuel up front and claim back business mileage at the advisory fuel rates.

# Chapter 3

# Capital Allowances

## What is a Capital Allowance?

Capital allowances are tax reliefs given to businesses for investment in plant and machinery. They can be set off against the profits made by the business to reduce its overall tax bill.

Plant and machinery has a very broad definition and includes cars and other vehicles.

Capital allowances can be claimed by a business under the following headings:

- Annual Investment Allowance
- Enhanced Capital Allowances
- Writing-down Allowances
- Balancing Allowances

We will now look at each of these in turn, focussing on how they apply to cars and other vehicles.

## Annual Investment Allowance

The Annual Investment Allowance (AIA) allows a business to claim 100% of the cost of an asset against tax in the year of purchase, but only up to a certain limit.

The limit is currently £100,000 but will fall to £25,000 in April 2012. If your expenditure on plant and machinery exceeds the AIA limit in any one year, you will only be able to claim the lower writing-down allowances on the balance.

The AIA only relates to expenditure incurred (or contracted) on or after 6th April each year (1st April for companies). If your year-end straddles this date and the AIA limit changes, you need to split your expenditure between the period before and the period after in order to determine how much AIA is available.

For most small businesses this is not an issue because even £25,000 is more than most spend on fixed assets.

However, it is worth noting that these limits also apply to groups of companies, not just single companies, so if your company is in a group it may not obtain its full allowance. You would need to split the AIA between all the companies in the group.

The AIA must also be adjusted if your accounting period is more or less than a year. For example, if it is only 6 months you would only be entitled to £50,000 for the 2011/12 tax year.

**Unfortunately the AIA specifically excludes cars. However, it does include vans and other vehicles.**

In other words, when your business buys a van the entire cost could qualify for immediate 100% tax relief.

As many vans cost a bit more than £25,000 any business that is planning to buy or replace one would be well advised to do before April 2012.

## Enhanced Capital Allowances

Enhanced Capital Allowances (ECAs) were introduced in April 2001 to encourage investment in energy-efficient assets.

Like the Annual Investment Allowance they allow a business to claim 100% of the cost of an asset against tax in the year of purchase.

The ECA regime was extended to cars with low carbon dioxide emissions purchased on or after 17 April 2002. The limit was originally set at 120 g/km but was reduced to 110 g/km when the tax break was extended for another 5 years in April 2008.

**Therefore businesses that buy cars with $CO_2$ emissions up to 110 g/km can potentially claim 100% tax relief.**

Unlike the Annual Investment Allowance, there is no limit on the amount you can claim for Enhanced Capital Allowances.

ECAs will continue to be allowed on qualifying vehicles until 31 March 2013. What happens after that date has not yet been announced, but if ECAs remain it would be surprising if the 110 g/km limit is not reduced to a much lower level.

## Sole Traders vs Companies

It's important to distinguish between the capital allowances enjoyed by company owners and the capital allowances enjoyed by sole traders and partnerships.

Sole traders and partnerships must reduce their capital allowances to reflect private use of the vehicle.

Take the example of a 'green' car that costs £20,000 and qualifies for an Enhanced Capital Allowance. If the car has 60% business use, the business can only claim tax relief on 60% of the cost, i.e. £12,000.

Companies do not have to reduce their capital allowances in this way. Instead the employee who uses the car privately pays income tax on a benefit in kind.

## Writing-down Allowances

Most cars generally qualify for writing-down allowances (WDAs) because they do not qualify for the Annual Investment Allowance or Enhanced Capital Allowances (except those with $CO_2$ emissions up to 110 g/km).

To understand how WDAs work, we first need to understand the concept of 'the pool'. All qualifying expenditure not allowed against tax in the year of purchase is credited to a plant and machinery pool.

The pool consists of a balance brought forward from the previous year plus purchases for the current year that do not qualify for the Annual Investment Allowance or Enhanced Capital Allowances.

You then need to deduct any sales proceeds or other income from disposals of plant and machinery, such as insurance claims.

A writing-down allowance is claimed on the amount remaining, which then reduces the value of the pool for next year.

## The Two Types of Pool

To make things even more complicated, there is not just one pool but two.

Certain assets must be credited to a separate pool, including:

- Cars with $CO_2$ emissions above 160 g/km
- Long life assets (more than 25 years), and
- Integral features in buildings, such as air conditioning.

That is because this type of expenditure only qualifies for WDAs at a reduced rate. Therefore they must be accounted for separately. To distinguish between the two, we refer to the "main pool" and the "special rate pool".

The writing-down allowance rate on the main pool is currently 20% and the rate on the special rate pool is 10%. These rates will fall to 18% and 8% respectively from April 2012.

WDAs are calculated on a 'reducing balance' basis, which means their value depends on the pool balance brought forward.

## How to Calculate WDAs

To illustrate how writing-down allowances work, the following example will show how much can be claimed in a situation where cars are bought and sold in the same year. Suppose that Alpha Ltd buys and sells the following cars during the 2011/12 tax year:

|  | $CO_2$ (g/km) | Purchase Cost | Sale Proceeds |
|---|---|---|---|
| **Purchases** | | | |
| Jaguar | 180 | £30,000 | |
| BMW | 140 | £25,000 | |
| | | | |
| **Disposals** | | | |
| Mercedes | 200 | | £15,000 |
| Audi | 160 | | £8,000 |

Alpha Limited has a brought forward balance of £50,000 on its main pool and £25,000 on its special rate pool. It spent £120,000 on other assets during the year, the first £100,000 of which qualified for the Annual Investment Allowance, and the balance of £20,000 was added to the main pool. Both the cars sold were acquired on or after 1st April 2009. The company's financial year end is 31 March. How much are its capital allowances for the year?

**Alpha Ltd**
**Capital Allowances Calculation**

|  | Main Pool | Special Pool |
|---|---|---|
| Balance brought forward | +£50,000 | +£25,000 |
| Jaguar |  | +£30,000 |
| BMW | +£25,000 |  |
| Mercedes |  | -£15,000 |
| Audi | -£8,000 |  |
| Other assets | +£20,000 |  |
| Balance allowable | £87,000 | £40,000 |
| WDA (20% & 10%) | -£17,400 | -£4,000 |
| Balance carried forward | +£69,600 | +£36,000 |

In summary the company can claim a tax deduction of £21,400 (£17,400 + £4,000) against its taxable profits.

### Small Pool Write-Offs

If the written down value of either the main pool or the special rate pool falls to £1,000 or less you can write off the residual balance against tax.

### Hybrid WDAs

If your financial year straddles 1st April 2012 (or 6th April 2012 for sole traders and partnerships) you will need to calculate *hybrid* writing-down allowances. This is because the writing-down allowances rates are being reduced in April 2012 from 20% to 18% (main pool) and from 10% to 8% (special rate pool). This is done by splitting the balance on a pro-rata basis.

Let's say that your year end is 31 December and the balance on the main pool is £40,000. You would have 91 days up to 31 March 2012 and 275 days after. You would therefore claim 25% of £40,000 at 20% and 75% of £40,000 at 18% and your hybrid writing-down allowance for the year would be £7,400.

## Pro-rata WDAs

It should be noted that if an accounting period is more or less than 12 months you must amend your writing-down allowances. For example, if an accounting period is 6 months, the writing-down allowance will be 50% of the annual equivalent. If it is 18 months, then it will be 150% of the annual equivalent.

## Private Use

Private use is only an issue when it comes to calculating capital allowances if you are a sole trader or a partnership. For limited companies there is no private use restriction because the car will probably be subject to company car tax.

The point about private use is that it must be calculated for each individual asset separately in order to determine the correct capital allowance. Consequently you cannot put assets with private use in the same pool. They must all go in their own individual pools.

As we shall see, this is very handy for sole traders and partnerships as it means they can claim a balancing allowance (potentially a big tax deduction) when the car is sold.

## Older Cars

Prior to April 2009 capital allowances were worked out differently for cars. It did not matter what the $CO_2$ emissions were. The only relevant issue was whether the car cost £12,000 or more. If so, the car would go in a separate pool by itself and its written-down value would be re-calculated each year. Once the car had been sold (or disposed of in some other way) the business would claim a balancing allowance on the remaining value after deducting sales proceeds.

This was known as the expensive cars rule. As many new cars now cost a lot more than £12,000 you can guess that this limit was frozen for a very long time!

However, if a company still has cars in its fleet purchased on or before 31$^{st}$ March 2009 for £12,000 or more, it must continue using the old rules for now.

If the car is still owned by the company on 1$^{st}$ April 2014, the written-down value will then have to be transferred to the main pool. Capital allowances are not allowed to exceed £3,000 per annum on any individual car – hence the need to put them all in separate pools.

Sole traders and partnerships must also follow the old rules on expensive cars purchased prior to 6$^{th}$ April 2009 but they are less relevant to them as in most cases their cars have to be pooled separately anyway in order to calculate the private use restriction.

## Balancing Allowances

Only sole traders and partnerships can now claim balancing allowances on cars purchased on or after 6$^{th}$ April 2009. Companies can only do so up to 31 March 2013 for cars purchased prior to 1$^{st}$ April 2009 that cost more than £12,000.

### Example

Suppose a sole trader bought a car with $CO_2$ emissions of 140 g/km on 1 March 2011 for £20,000. The car has 40% private use.

He prepares accounts up to 31 December each year and sells the car on 31 October 2014 for £5,000.

How much is his balancing allowance?

| Year | Transaction | Written-down value | Private Use Restriction | Capital Allowance |
|-------|-------------|---------------------|--------------------------|--------------------|
| 2011 | Purchase of car | +£20,000 | | |
| | WDA at 20% | -£4,000 | 40% | £2,400 |
| | Balance carried forward | +£16,000 | | |
| 2012 | Hybrid WDA at 20% and 18% | -£2,960 | 40% | £1,776 |
| | Balance carried forward | +£13,040 | | |
| 2013 | WDA at 18% | -£2,347 | 40% | £1,408 |
| | Balance carried forward | +£10,693 | | |
| 2014 | Disposal proceeds | -£5,000 | | |
| | Remaining value | £5,693 | | |
| | Balancing allowance | -£5,693 | 40% | £3,416 |
| | Total capital allowances | | | £9,000 |

In this example the business claims a balancing allowance of £3,416 when the car is sold. This can be described as a catch-up tax deduction because it makes up the tax relief that was not given when the car was being used by the business.

Note that the total capital allowances of £9,000 are equivalent to the actual net capital cost of £15,000 (£20,000 purchase price less £5,000 disposal proceeds) x 60% business use.

Also, it is necessary to calculate a hybrid WDA for 2012 as it straddles two tax years where the rate has changed. Lastly, there is no WDA in the year of disposal, as a balancing allowance is given instead.

If the car has no private use or is purchased by a company, it would be added to the main pool. When it is sold the sales proceeds will be deducted from the pool balance. The remaining value will then attract annual writing-down allowances which means it may take many years before full tax relief is given.

Sadly companies cannot claim a balancing allowance any more when they sell cars, unless the car was purchased before 1st April 2009 and cost £12,000 or more.

**Claiming balancing allowances is one of the few remaining tax advantages enjoyed by sole traders and partnerships over limited companies. There is no limit to the amount that can be claimed as a balancing allowance.**

However it is important to point out that sole traders and partnerships must use their cars both privately and for business purposes if they wish to enjoy balancing allowances when they are sold.

So if your car is used mainly for business purposes, make sure you take it to the shops a few times so there is some private use.

## Balancing Charges

In theory there could also be a *balancing charge* if the original cost net of sale proceeds is less than the amount claimed in capital allowances. However, in most cases the car would depreciate at a faster rate unless perhaps it is a classic car with some investment potential.

Of course, there is one situation where there will always be a balancing charge and that is on cars with $CO_2$ emissions of 110 g/km or less (or 120 g/km if bought prior to April 2008).

Because a business is entitled to claim a 100% Enhanced Capital Allowance on such cars, the sale proceeds on disposal will be taxed as a balancing charge.

Similarly, vans that qualify for the 100% Annual Investment Allowance could be subject to balancing charges when sold.

# Chapter 4

# Pool Cars

## Qualifying Conditions

A lot of company owners ask whether they can escape company car tax if they have a pool car.

Pool cars (or vans) are not taxable benefits for the employees who drive them, so it is definitely worth taking the trouble to ensure that company vehicles can be classified as such if possible.

Unfortunately the rules are very strict and there must be no private mileage whatsoever, apart from merely incidental journeys. A car will only be classified as a pool car if it satisfies *all* of the following five conditions:

- The car was made available to, and actually used, by more than one employee

- The car was made available to employees by reason of their employment

- The car was not ordinarily used by one employee to the exclusion of the others

- Any private use was merely incidental to an employee's other use of it (in the same tax year)

- The car was not *normally* kept overnight at or near the residence of any employee who uses it

These are really tough conditions. A car used primarily by one employee for business reasons only cannot be treated as a pool vehicle. It also theoretically means that private use by one employee renders the vehicle taxable for everyone else who uses it too!

Fortunately, occasional private use of a pool car is forgiven by the taxman provided the employees in question reimburse the company for their deemed benefit. It will also help if there are written contracts forbidding employees from making private use of pooled cars.

All the same, it would be wise not to let it happen too often as, strictly speaking, it would then be necessary for each individual employee to prove that the vehicle was not available for private use for the whole tax year in order to avoid it going on their P11Ds as a taxable benefit.

That would be an almost impossible task if the vehicle had previously been made available to them in that tax year because it is the availability that counts, not their actual use of the vehicle (with the exception of vans).

## Private Use

A certain amount of private use is permitted in pool cars provided it is incidental. Incidental private use is based on the main reason for the journey. If the vehicle was being used for a business trip and the driver stopped on the way for a private errand, this would be regarded as incidental.

However, if the driver used it to do his weekly shopping and stopped on the way to meet a customer, the opposite would apply and it would be the business use that was incidental.

Employees are allowed to take vehicles home in order to make an early start on a business trip the next day, but this must not happen too often.

Overnight parking at or near an employee's home is generally prohibited for pool cars.

You cannot even get round this restriction by claiming that there are no parking facilities near the company premises or that the car might get broken into or damaged by vandals.

You may get away with employees parking the vehicle near their own homes if this happened on less than 60% of the total number of nights during the period under review. Unfortunately, the 60% test is only a rule of thumb and does not have the force of law. If one or more employees did get near the 60% test, it is unlikely that all of their home-to-work journeys would be regarded as incidental private use.

However, there is one possible loophole. If the vehicle is parked overnight on premises occupied by the person who is making it available to other employees (eg a director), then the 5$^{th}$ condition is met. Therefore, a sole director could theoretically park a pool car at his own home provided it was actually used for business purposes by other employees on a regular basis.

## Availability for Use

Availability for use must be taken into consideration if the vehicle fails any of the five conditions. A car or van is unavailable for use if:

- It is physically incapable of being driven (e.g., it is in a garage undergoing repairs), or

- An employee is unable to gain access to the car (e.g., they do not have the keys and cannot require someone else to hand them over)

However, if the vehicle was available both before and after the period in question, it must have been unavailable for at least 30 consecutive days, otherwise there is no reduction in the car/van benefit charge.

A car or van is *not* unavailable for use merely because the employee in question is banned from driving, away on holiday or on sick leave.

This would mean that it was the employee who was unavailable to drive the car or van, not the other way round.

Likewise, a vehicle does not become unavailable simply because there is no current road tax, insurance or MOT certificate. However, if one or more of these situations results in a car being physically withdrawn from an employee, then the unavailability test would be met.

## Pool Car Recommendations

If you are thinking of designating a car or van as a pooled vehicle, it would be wise to keep the following records:

- Detailed mileage log recording each individual journey

- Destination and purpose of each journey

- Overnight parking log showing all employees living nearby

- Key log showing who was in charge of the vehicle and on what dates

- All transfers of keys to be authorised and signed off

- Regular reconciliation of the odometer to the mileage log for each vehicle

- All drivers to sign contracts stating that no private use is allowed

- Fuel bills to be checked against mileage records to ensure they look compatible

- All records to be reviewed by a responsible person at least monthly and any anomalies reported

This may seem onerous but it should avoid any problems with the pooled status and either eliminate or substantially reduce any tax liability that may arise.

If a vehicle does look as though it may lose its pooled status, all relevant employees should be informed immediately and warned of the possible tax implications.

Persons at risk of incurring tax liabilities should either get the chance to waive all future use of the vehicle or be compensated accordingly if it was not their fault, given that any private use or overnight parking by them whatsoever in that tax year would make them liable to a car benefit charge.

# Chapter 5

# Vans

## What is a Van?

According to Section 115 of ITEPA 2003, a van is a mechanically propelled road vehicle that:

- Is a goods vehicle primarily suited for the conveyance of goods or burden of any description
- Has a design weight not exceeding 3,500 kilograms; and
- Has (or is meant to have) at least 4 wheels

Passengers are not classed as a burden (not even chauffeur-driven MPs) so a minibus is not a van.

Anything exceeding 3,500 kilograms is not a van but a heavy goods vehicle. These are non-taxable provided they are not used wholly or mainly for private use. Private use is unlikely to occur with an HGV although, unlike vans, you must count home-to-work travel as private use.

## Tax Advantages of Vans

### VAT

Vans are generally very tax efficient. For starters, unlike cars, VAT can be recovered when you buy a van (provided your business is VAT registered, of course).

### Capital Allowances

Secondly, vans attract higher capital allowances than cars. Vans qualify for the Annual Investment Allowance, so the business is entitled to a 100% tax write-off in the year of purchase, providing the business has not used up its allowance for the year.

The Annual Investment Allowance applies to both new and second-hand assets, so the 100% tax write-off is also available if you buy a second-hand van.

### Benefit-in-Kind Charges

Sole traders and partnerships must reduce their VAT and capital allowance claims proportionally if there is any private use of the van.

Company owners do not have to reduce their capital allowance claim if there is private use of the vehicle. Instead the employee who uses the van privately must pay tax on the van benefit in kind.

When it comes to calculating the taxable benefit for vans, $CO_2$ emissions are irrelevant. The taxable benefit on private use of a company van is a flat £3,000 per annum, which is usually less than for a car with equivalent $CO_2$ emissions.

So a higher-rate taxpayer would typically pay £1,200 per year in extra income tax (£3,000 x 40% income tax) and the company would pay £414 in national insurance (£3,000 x 13.8%).

### What Is Private Use?

The benefit-in-kind charge on a car applies if there is **any** private use, even if the car is simply available for private use and even if the car is only used to travel between home and work.

For vans the rules on private use are less onerous than for a car because:

- It is actual use that counts rather than the availability of the van;
- Insignificant private use can be ignored; and
- Home-to-work travel and overnight parking near your own home are not taxable.

So a director whose only private usage of a van is commuting from home to work will not face a benefit-in-kind charge.

For tax purposes, *insignificant* private use of a van is notably less stringent than *incidental* private use of a pool car.

With pool cars private use must only happen during a business trip for it to be incidental. But for a van you can do things like take rubbish to the dump once or twice a year, regularly take a slight detour to drop your children off at school on the way to work or dental appointments on the way home from work.

You can also use the van as often as you like to travel between home and work, even if that would be defined as ordinary commuting (i.e. private travel) for any other purpose. It follows that overnight parking near your home is also non-taxable. Neither of these private uses is allowed for pool cars other than in exceptional circumstances.

The conditions for *insignificant* private use are:

- It is very much the exception to the normal use of the van
- It is intermittent and irregular; and
- It lasts for only short periods of time on odd occasions during the year.

Unacceptable uses would be taking the van on holiday, using the van outside work for social activities or regularly taking it to a supermarket to do your shopping. If you want to do anything like this, it would probably scupper the van's tax-free status for the whole tax year.

There is no tax charge for mobile phones fitted to the van or reimbursements for the cost of parking at or near your place of work. This parking concession applies to cars as well and is one of the few tax-free perks still existing.

### *Fuel*

If fuel is provided to directors or employees for private use there is a further benefit-in-kind charge. For cars the taxable charge can be up to £6,580 per year:

$$£18,800 \times 35\% = £6,580$$

For a 40% taxpayer the tax on this amount is £2,632 and for the company the national insurance cost is £908.

For vans the taxation of private fuel is much more generous. The private fuel charge is just £550 per annum, costing a 40% taxpayer employee £220 in income tax and costing the company just £76 in national insurance.

## Double Cab Pick-ups

There are a number of vehicles known as double cab pick-ups that are treated as vans rather than cars for tax purposes.

The tax advantages are obvious as the tax regime for vans is more attractive than it is for cars, although most owners probably buy vans for their ability to transport both goods and people rather than for tax reasons.

Double cab pick-ups are usually more of a lifestyle choice, although the major manufacturers recognise that the company car market is a big contributor to sales.

What is a double cab pick-up? A vehicle of this sort normally has:

- A front passenger cab that contains a second row of seats
- Four doors capable of being opened independently; and
- An uncovered pick-up area behind the passenger cab

Typical examples are the Ford Ranger, the Mitsubishi L200 and the Isuzu Rodeo.

The vehicle can get away with being treated as a van rather than a car if the predominant reason for their construction is to carry goods or burden rather than passengers. It does not matter what they are actually used for later. This will depend on various factors relating to their construction and HM Revenue & Customs has stated that it is not possible to come up with a single categorisation for all double cab pick-ups.

**However, any such vehicle that has a payload of at least 1 tonne (1,000 kg) will definitely be accepted as a van in line with the definitions used for VAT purposes.**

Payload is defined as gross vehicle weight, less unoccupied kerb weight.

If a hard top has been added to the pick-up area this must also be deducted. Under a separate agreement between HMRC and the Society of Motor Manufacturers and Traders (SMMT), a hard top consisting of metal, fibre glass or similar material, with or without windows, is accorded a generic weight of 45 kg.

Therefore, the addition of a hard top to a double cab pick-up with an ex-works payload of 1,010 kg will convert the vehicle into a car as the net payload would be reduced to 965 kg. Under this agreement, the weight of all other optional accessories is disregarded. Care needs to be taken when looking at brochures produced by manufacturers as payload is sometimes defined differently.

Do your research if you decide to buy a double cab pick-up principally to save tax. The salesman may be quick to point out the tax efficiency of a particular vehicle but it is only HM Revenue & Customs' opinion that counts, so don't fall for the sales patter.

Don't bother asking your local tax office as they are instructed not to give definite answers on individual vehicles. They will merely refer you to the general advice on the HMRC website.

## Recommendations for Vans

We would suggest that you keep some or all of the following records for company vans:

- Detailed mileage log recording each individual journey
- Destination and purpose of each journey
- A note of the odometer readings on every garage bill
- Regular reconciliation of the odometer to the mileage log for each vehicle
- All drivers to sign contracts stating that no significant private use is allowed
- Fuel bills to be checked against mileage records to ensure they look compatible
- All records to be reviewed by a responsible person at least monthly and any anomalies reported

Of course, it is notoriously difficult trying to get van drivers to keep mileage logs and it may be necessary to work it all out later from estimates.

But tax can be a bit like the hangman's noose – the prospect of it concentrates the mind wonderfully! If you explain to your van drivers that they will get clobbered for £600 tax a year (or even double that for high earners) if they make any private journeys outside the rules, most of them will try to make sure this does not happen. Or at least they will try to make sure you never find out if they do!

For regular employees a clause in their contract barring private use apart from home-to-work travel is a must. That will prove to the taxman that the intent is there. Regular checks of the odometer are also important as it proves you are serious about enforcing that rule. You should also keep records of conversations with van drivers regarding any anomalies and receipts for fuel expenses. It all might seem a bit pedantic to them but it is for their own good!

If you trade through your own company and drive the van yourself, it is up to you to keep your own records if you want the taxman to believe that there was never any private use. A good mileage log is vital.

Otherwise you will probably end up trying to prove that it was only ever used for business from the fuel bills, which is not a very precise method. If your odometer is in line with the fuel receipts for the whole tax year and your known business journeys are in line with the fuel bills, then you may stand a chance if push comes to shove, but don't bet on it.

The safest option is to keep a mileage log in the van and update it for every single journey, even if it was only a couple of miles down the road. Even a notebook on the dashboard will do.

Chapter 6

# Running Costs

## Fuel

Fuel is usually the largest cost associated with running a car. From a tax planning point of view it is also the trickiest to deal with.

### Company Owners

The big decision company owners have to make is whether to have a company car or not. Chapter 8 explores this subject in detail.

### Without Company Car

If you do not have a company car and use your own car for business journeys, the company can make tax-free payments to you at the approved mileage rates:

- 45p per business mile for first 10,000 miles per tax year
- 25p thereafter

You can also claim an extra 5p per mile for each passenger that travels with you for business reasons.

The company can then claim the amount it pays you as a tax deduction. For example, if you travel 5,000 miles during the year on business the company can pay you £2,250 tax free and the company can claim corporation tax relief on £2,250.

Employers do not have to pay as much as 45p per mile. If the employer pays less, the employee is entitled to claim back the difference on his or her tax return.

For example, suppose an employee drives 15,000 miles in his own car and receives 30p per mile from his employer. This would amount to £4,500. However, the taxman would have allowed him to claim up to £5,750 (10,000 x 45p + 5,000 x 25p), so he can claim the shortfall of £1,250 against tax. Therefore, if you pay tax at 40% you would get a rebate of £500.

Should your employer pay you *more* than the approved tax free mileage rates, then the opposite would apply and you would be taxed on the excess. Any such payments should be reported on your annual P11D, which is a form summarising your expenses and benefits. Mileage expenses should never appear on this form unless they exceed the tax free rates.

### With Company Car

If you do opt for a company car, then you must decide whether to let the company pay for your private fuel. Chapter 10 deals with this issue but the answer is almost invariably No.

It is usually best for company car users to pay for all the fuel personally and claim back business mileage from the company at the advisory fuel rates. These rates change frequently and can be found here:

www.hmrc.gov.uk/cars/advisory_fuel_current.htm

The amount paid to you by the company is tax free in your hands and the company can claim the amount as a tax deduction.

At the time of writing the average rate was around 18p per mile. That's much lower than the 45p that can claimed by employees who use their own cars for business.

The reason for the difference is that the 45p rate is supposed to cover ALL motoring costs, including fuel, depreciation, and servicing, whereas the 18p rate only covers fuel.

It is usually best if the company does not pay for private fuel. Chapter 16 looks at some of the common pitfalls that may trap the unwary and result in an unexpected tax charge on a fuel benefit.

It is very easy to fall foul of the rules and the safest option is to pay for all fuel yourself and then claim business mileage from your company.

For a company with employees driving company cars as part of their jobs, fuel cards are probably a necessity and they would have to be on an account in the employer's name. In that case, the employer needs to have robust procedures for the reimbursement of private mileage in order to avoid a benefit-in-kind charge.

That means employees have to keep detailed mileage logs that are regularly reconciled to the odometer. There should also be clauses in staff contracts making it clear that private mileage must be reimbursed as soon as possible, especially at the end of the tax year. This will at least show that the employer has a policy in place and that a legal obligation on the employee exists. All you need to do then is prove that this policy was carried out in practice.

One difficulty with private fuel reimbursements on company cars is that they must be at least as high as the advisory fuel rates published by HM Revenue & Customs, unless you can prove otherwise, which is rather difficult.

It may be easier for employers to set reimbursements some way above the advisory fuel rates, say at 25p per mile for cars up to 2000cc, so there is no danger of reimbursements falling short. The extra could be justified as a contribution towards other running costs, although this is strictly unofficial and should never be quantified or else it would be an easy target for any visiting PAYE inspector. Reimbursements for private fuel should never be mixed up with other employee payments, such as private use contributions, insurance or maintenance costs.

### Sole Traders and Partnerships

Fuel costs are easier to deal with for sole traders and partnerships. For them there is no question of a taxable benefit in kind arising on private fuel (unless they give cars to their employees for their private use).

However, sole traders and partnerships must reduce the amount claimed for tax purposes to reflect private use of the vehicle. For example, if the vehicle is used 60% for business purposes then only 60% of the fuel costs can be claimed as a business tax deduction.

For sole traders and partnerships with turnover under £73,000, the main tax planning decision is whether to claim the business portion of the vehicle's running costs or the approved tax-free mileage rates.

Chapter 9 examines which method is best.

Whichever method is chosen, it is necessary to keep mileage records. In theory you could simply estimate the private use percentage after your first year of trading and use the same percentage every year (unless it changes significantly).

You could even calculate private use using a different method such as the number of journeys, time spent, etc.

However, the standard way of splitting business and private use of a car is by mileage, even if the figures are only estimated. The taxman would normally expect you to keep a mileage log as part of your accounting records and may ask to see it.

### All VAT-Registered Businesses

Finally, all VAT-registered businesses need to decide on their policy for recovering VAT on fuel.

Chapter 11 analyses this subject in great detail, and the only thing that is worth repeating again here is that, according to the official rules, you *must* keep the fuel receipts.

By that I mean proper VAT receipts, not the credit card slips. This little addition to the mountain of red tape we have to cope with these days is courtesy of our friends in Brussels, who back in 2005 ruled that the UK was in breach of EU rules by allowing input tax recoveries on fuel without VAT receipts.

Luckily most fuel station attendants nowadays are trained to ask if you want a VAT receipt. Your employees should always say Yes and keep the receipts somewhere safe, not screwed-up in the back of the glove compartment. You never know when a VAT inspector might ask to see them.

# Insurance

Next to fuel, insurance is probably the most expensive item in the list of running costs, especially if you or your car falls into a high risk category.

## *Company Owners*

The good news for company owners is that insurance is 100% deductible against corporation tax and does not represent a taxable benefit on you as the employee, even if you get a booklet of money-off coupons courtesy of the insurance company!

## *Sole Traders and Partnerships*

Sole traders and partnerships can only claim a proportion of insurance based on business use. For example, if your insurance premium is £600 a year and you use the car 60% for business, you can claim £360 against tax.

Employees, on the other hand, can claim nothing on their income tax returns for motor insurance as it is covered by the 45p tax-free mileage rate, even if they use their cars for business.

I am occasionally asked if it is OK to claim additional premiums for business use against tax on the grounds that the extra cover was only required for work purposes. The answer is usually No for the simple reason that you would normally claim the tax free mileage rates for business use and they specifically cover all running costs.

Self-employed persons who claim tax relief on the business portion of their motoring costs would be able to claim 100% of the additional premium provided it is quantifiable (ie it was quoted separately by the insurer). The rest of the premium would then be apportioned between business and private use as normal.

As far as VAT is concerned, insurance premiums are always exempt. There is no VAT to pay on insurance policies so there is no input tax to recover. There is a thing called Insurance Premium Tax but sadly you cannot claim this back from the taxman.

## All Businesses

One thing you should always do with insurance, whether you are a sole trader, a partnership or a company, is only claim for the proportion of the premium that relates to your accounting period.

Therefore, if your insurance renewal date is 31 December but your accounts are for the year ended 31 March, you should claim 3/12ths of the current year's premium and 9/12ths of the previous year's premium.

# Road Tax

As all motorists know, road tax (or Vehicle Excise Duty) is an annual charge levied on almost all cars that are kept or used on the public road. The only way you can avoid road tax (unless your car is one of the few that are exempt) is to declare SORN (Statutory Off-Road Notification) and keep it off the road. Obviously this is only a short-term measure, for example if your car is being repaired or nobody is driving it for some reason.

VED is now levied in bands according to the $CO_2$ emissions. The 2011/12 rates are as follows:

| VED Band | $CO_2$ (g/km) | 1st Year Rate | Standard Rate |
|----------|---------------|---------------|---------------|
| A | Up to 100 | - | - |
| B | 101-110 | - | £20 |
| C | 111-120 | - | £30 |
| D | 121-130 | - | £95 |
| E | 131-140 | £115 | £115 |
| F | 141-150 | £130 | £130 |
| G | 151-165 | £165 | £165 |
| H | 166-175 | £265 | £190 |
| I | 176-185 | £315 | £210 |
| J | 186-200 | £445 | £245 |
| K | 201-225 | £580 | £260 |
| L | 226-255 | £790 | £445 |
| M | Over 255 | £1,000 | £460 |

These rates apply to all cars registered since 1 March 2001. For cars registered before this date, VED is based on engine size as follows:

| Engine Capacity | Duty |
| --- | --- |
| Up to 1549cc | £130 |
| Above 1549cc | £215 |

The first year rate is included within the list price for the car when it is bought new. This should be treated as an expense in the year of purchase rather than as part of the price of the car.

## Vans

Vans are taxed differently to cars as they are not designated a VED band based on $CO_2$ emissions. Instead, the tax depends on when the van was first registered and (for older vehicles) their engine size.

For the 2011/12 tax year VED on vans will be either £130 or £210. Vans registered prior to 1 March 2001 are taxed at £130 per annum if the engine size is up to 1549cc or £210 per annum if above that figure.

If the van is registered between 1 March 2001 and 28 February 2003, it will be taxed at £210 per annum, whatever its engine size. Vans registered from 1 March 2003 onwards will have either a Euro 4 or Euro 5 rating and are taxed at a flat £130 per annum.

## Sole Traders and Partnerships

VED is a tax deductible trading expense but is covered by the approved tax free mileage rates, so if you are claiming the mileage rates you cannot claim for VED too.

If you do not claim the mileage rates then you should only claim a proportion of VED based on business use.

## Company Owners

Companies can claim 100% of VED payments if a car is treated as a taxable benefit on an employee. All other cars owned by a company should have 100% business use anyway.

## Maintenance

Repair and maintenance costs can be claimed against tax as business expenses.

### *Sole Traders and Partnerships*

As with fuel and insurance, repairs and maintenance are covered by the tax free mileage rates so cannot be claimed in addition to these.

However, if a sole trader or partnership eschews the mileage rates and opts to claim the actual costs instead, they should disallow a certain proportion for private use.

### *Employees Using their Own Cars*

Employees using their own cars for business trips do not have this option – they must claim the tax free mileage rates instead.

A common question is whether you can claim 100% of the repair costs (in addition to the mileage rates) if your car is damaged whilst on a business trip? Unfortunately the answer is No.

### *Company Owners*

Companies can claim 100% of their repairs and maintenance on cars and other vehicles, as they will normally be taxed as company cars.

There is no additional taxable benefit on the employee for repairs and maintenance, as there is with private fuel, although anything that is an improvement to the car, such as accessories, should be added to the list price in order to calculate the benefit-in-kind.

### VAT on Repairs and Maintenance

VAT can be claimed back on repairs and maintenance by most businesses if they are registered for VAT.

Exceptions are partially exempt businesses (such as banks and insurance companies), who are restricted on the amount of input tax they can reclaim, and any business that uses the VAT flat rate scheme.

It is also not possible to claim back VAT on repairs and maintenance for an employee's own car, even if the employer paid the bill.

It is perhaps surprising that a business can claim back 100% of the VAT on repairs and maintenance regardless of the amount of private use. The only condition is that there must be at least *some* business use.

Therefore, sole traders and partnerships should make sure they do at least one business trip a year in order to claim back all the VAT on their garage bills.

## Loan Finance

### Sole Traders and Partnerships

It is not often realised that finance costs can be claimed by self-employed persons against tax *in addition* to the tax-free mileage rates if a car is used for business.

Finance costs are not covered by the approved tax free mileage rates.

If you are a sole trader or work through a partnership and use your own car in the business, you can claim part of the interest on any related loan on your tax return. How much you can claim of course depends on the business use proportion.

For a sole trader or partner, this can make a big difference when deciding whether to claim mileage or actual running costs. If you can claim the finance charges on top of mileage, you may be far more inclined to opt for the mileage rates.

### *Employees Using their Own Cars*

Sadly the same is not true for employees. If you use your own car for business trips you cannot claim a proportion of loan finance on top of mileage, even if it is your own company.

### *Purpose of Loan*

It should be noted that the loan must have been *used* to buy the car, irrespective of what its original purpose may have been. If you bought the car on hire purchase or under a finance lease, the interest on that would qualify as well. For operating leases the monthly rentals are normally tax-deductible anyway, unless the $CO_2$ emissions are higher than 160 g/km, in which case you must deduct 15%.

Proving that a loan was used to buy a car may not be so easy if it was non-specific, although interest payments are generally allowable against tax anyway, so this should not make any difference at the end of the day. If the loan was for business purposes, then the interest can be claimed against tax.

## Parking & Tolls

Any costs that are directly related to a business trip can be claimed against tax in full, even if you are already claiming the tax free mileage rates.

The main items covered by this rule are parking fees, road/bridge tolls and congestion charges. This rule also applies to employees using their cars for work, so they can be reimbursed by their employers for these costs without a taxable benefit arising.

Of course, you may not have the receipt for the parking as they are often swallowed by the barriers before they let you out. Therefore you should record exactly when and where you parked to avoid any issues with lack of receipts.

It is worth noting that the provision by your employer of parking facilities at or near your place of work is a tax-free benefit. Your employer can also reimburse you for parking at or near work without a taxable benefit arising, even if you are not on a business trip.

It does not have to be an assigned parking space in a designated area and there are no rules on how close to your place of work it has to be.

Therefore, you can claim for the cost of an annual parking permit against your business profits. However, you would probably not get away with claims for parking near your home, as then there would be a dual purpose.

Local authorities are now empowered to raise taxes on employers for workplace parking, which may encourage some to pass it on to their employees. However, this does not apply to car parks owned by third parties, so your employer could hire spaces and allocate them to individuals. In fact, this is often used in conjunction with a salary sacrifice scheme to reduce tax and national insurance.

## *VAT*

VAT can be recovered on parking fees although it is not often clear whether the operator is VAT registered. You should be able to see their VAT registration number on the receipts.

There is definitely no VAT on street parking operated by local authorities, however. There is also no VAT on congestion zone charges or on bridge tolls run by public bodies, although tolls charged by private operators are normally standard rated.

## Penalties

Penalties for motoring offences often cause confusion as far as the tax implications are concerned.

What happens if the penalty is incurred whilst the driver is on company business and the employer pays it on his/her behalf? Is there a tax liability on the employee? And can the employer claim parking fines against profits in their own tax computations?

I've lost count of the number of clients down the years who have tried to put parking fines through the business. Invariably they prompt a wide range of hard luck stories. Some of them have almost had me in tears (of laughter).

Sometimes, however, the boot has been on the other foot. In particular, some of my clients got to nicknaming me Sidney Bernstein a few years ago because of all the parking tickets I picked up whilst visiting them.

They didn't mean the media baron. They were referring to the wacky accountant in Beverley Hills Cop who was arrested for having 25 unpaid parking tickets. Often I would overstay my allotted time by a few minutes and look out the window to see a parking attendant already hovering over my car, writing out the ticket, to gales of laughter from the staff in the office.

Parking tickets and similar fines are an easy target for tax inspectors on PAYE compliance visits. The usual rule is that penalties incurred for parking offences, speeding, jumping red lights, etc, are the responsibility of whoever happened to be driving the vehicle at the time, and any reimbursement by the employer will give rise to a taxable benefit. It does not matter if they happened to be on company business at the time.

### When Employers Can Pay Fines

However, there are some circumstances where this rule does not apply: when parking tickets are fixed to a car owned by the employer (or posted to the employer's address). The employer can then pay it without any taxable benefit arising on the employee, although the fine would have to be disallowed in the employer's tax computation. I stress that the car must be owned by the employer. This does not work for cars owned by employees.

If the car is owned by the employer but the penalty notice is actually handed to the employee by a police officer or parking attendant, then the employer cannot pay it on his/her behalf without a taxable benefit arising.

However, if the employer decides to pay it on behalf of the employee anyway, they would *not* have to disallow it in their own tax computation.

So the lesson for company car drivers seems to be this – never accept a penalty notice from a parking attendant. Always make them fix it to the car, even if they have to run down the road after you. I would not advise anyone to try that with the police though!

If an employee voluntarily pays a penalty notice and the employer reimburses him/her for it, then it becomes a taxable benefit on the employee. In that case, the employer would be allowed to claim a tax deduction for it. Most employers require their company car drivers to pay any parking tickets or speeding fines themselves though, so tax issues should not arise.

### Company Owner-Managers

There is an alternative way of dealing with parking tickets and other motoring penalties if you work through your own limited company. Say you use your own car in the business and pay a parking ticket out of the company account. Your accountant comes along and tells you it should go on your P11D. If you wish, you could just debit it to your director's loan account instead. Then, the company has not really paid it on your behalf at all. It has simply given you a loan to pay it, or offset it against money it owes you. Obviously you need to watch your loan account as overdrawn balances in excess of £5,000 are taxable, but it will prevent a taxable benefit arising on the penalty.

### Sole Traders and Partnerships

For sole traders and partnerships, the car would be owned by you personally, not the business. However, you are the proprietor of the business, not an employee. Consequently, no taxable benefit on you can arise if it is paid by the business. It would simply be disallowed against income tax on your trading profits.

### Employees

There is a general rule that penalties cannot be claimed against tax even if they are incurred in the course of trade, such as when unloading goods or on business trips. However, as mentioned above, there is an exception for penalties paid on behalf of employees, as then the employer would be discharging a liability that belonged to someone else. If this was in the course of trade then it would be allowable.

The fine is either taxable on the employee or disallowable for the employer – never both.

Therefore, if a penalty notice is reported on an employee's P11D or goes through the payroll, the employer does not have to disallow it in their tax computation. If no taxable benefit has to be reported, then by definition it is the employer who is liable and the fine must be disallowed against tax.

### Who is to blame?

For cars owned by an employer, you should always distinguish between penalties that are issued because of the way someone is driving a car and those that relate to the car itself. If a penalty is issued because the tax disc has expired or the car has defective tyres, for example, the employer will always be liable even if the penalty notice was handed to the driver. As such, these kinds of penalties are always disallowed against tax.

The best policy of course is to try and avoid penalty notices in the first place. Easier said than done in this day and age, but if you do incur them always make a note in your accounting records of the car it relates to, the name of the driver and the circumstances so that the tax treatment can be verified.

# Part 2

# How to Save Tax on Your Car

Chapter 7

# Initial Considerations

## Relevant Factors

This is by far the most important part of the book and probably the reason you have bought it. Saving tax is something that most business people have a keen interest in and cars are one of the most fertile areas for sensible tax planning.

Indeed, you might even have skipped the previous chapters and come straight to these pages in search of immediate inspiration. However, it will be hard to follow the logic and calculations given in this chapter without an understanding of the various tax rules relating to cars in business.

If you have diligently read the whole book up to this point, you will be keenly aware of the various factors that can affect the tax on your car when you use it in your business. Let us remind ourselves of what these are.

We have identified 27 different factors that, in some way or other, may be relevant to the key decisions you will make with regard to your car and the use you make of it in your business. These are listed in the table below and the particular area they are relevant to is shown alongside for handy reference. We also show which ones are relevant to company cars (nearly all of them) and which to cars that are owned by you personally.

We would stress that the Company Car column is only relevant to those who work through their own limited companies. Anyone who is a sole trader or works through a partnership (including a Limited Liability Partnership) will only be concerned with the Own Car column.

|    |                         |         | Company Car | Own Car |
| -- | ----------------------- | ------- | ----------- | ------- |
| 1  | Manufacturer's list price | BIK     | X           |         |
| 2  | Purchase price          | CA      | X           | X       |
| 3  | List price of accessories | BIK   | X           |         |
| 4  | The use of the car      | BIK     | X           |         |
| 5  | $CO_2$ emissions        | BIK/CA  | X           | X       |
| 6  | Taxable % of list price | BIK     | X           |         |
| 7  | Flat rate fuel benefit  | BIK     | X           |         |
| 8  | Fuel type               | BIK/CA  | X           | X       |
| 9  | Fuel costs              | EXP     | X           | X       |
| 10 | Capital contributions   | BIK/CA  | X           |         |
| 11 | Personal use contribs   | BIK/EXP | X           |         |
| 12 | Fuel consumption        | EXP     | X           | X       |
| 13 | Other running costs      | EXP     | X           | X       |
| 14 | Mileage per tax year    | EXP     | X           | X       |
| 15 | Business mileage        | EXP     | X           | X       |
| 16 | Availability private use | BIK    | X           |         |
| 17 | Advisory fuel rates     | EXP/VAT | X           | X       |
| 18 | Approved mileage rates  | EXP     |             | X       |
| 19 | Engine size             | EXP/VAT | X           | X       |
| 20 | Resale value            | CA      | X           | X       |
| 21 | Period of ownership     | BIK/EXP | X           | X       |
| 22 | Your marginal tax rate  | ITAX    | X           | X       |
| 23 | Class 1A NI rate        | BIK     | X           |         |
| 24 | Class 4 NI rate         | ITAX    |             | X       |
| 25 | Corporation tax rate    | CTAX    | X           |         |
| 26 | VAT fuel scale charges  | VAT     | X           | X       |
| 27 | VAT standard rate       | VAT/CA  | X           | X       |

BIK – Benefit in Kind  
CA – Capital Allowances  
EXP – Expenses  

VAT – Value Added Tax  
ITAX – Income Tax  
CTAX – Corporation Tax  

A quick glance at this list shows that there are many more factors on the Company Car side than on the Own Car side. In fact, all but two of these factors apply to company cars, which is mainly due to the complexity of the benefit-in-kind rules.

## Why Are these Factors Relevant?

Let's briefly recap why each of these factors is relevant.

*1 – Manufacturer's List Price*
The basis on which company cars are taxed – the higher the list price the higher the tax.

*2 – Purchase Price*
The basis on which capital allowances are claimed – the higher the purchase price the higher the capital allowances.

*3 – List Price of Accessories*
Increases the tax liability on company cars.

*4 – The Use of the Car*
Removes the tax liability of company cars in certain circumstances; eg disabled drivers, pool cars, demonstration cars.

*5 – CO$_2$ Emissions*
Determines the taxable percentage of the list price on company cars, the annual value of capital allowances and the tax relief on lease rentals.

*6 – Taxable Percentage of List Price*
Determines the tax liability on company cars - the higher the percentage the higher the tax.

*7 – Flat Rate Fuel Benefit*
Determines the tax liability on fuel provided by employers for company cars.

*8 – Fuel Type*
Influences the taxable percentage for company cars and the annual value of capital allowances.

*9 – Fuel Costs*
Influences the tax efficiency of getting your company to pay for all fuel.

*10 – Capital Contributions*
Reduce the tax liability on a company car but also reduce capital allowances.

*11 – Personal Use Contributions*
Reduce the tax liability on a company car but also reduce expenses allowable against corporation tax.

*12 – Fuel Consumption*
Determines the tax efficiency of mileage payments compared with actual fuel costs.

*13 – Other Running Costs*
The higher the running costs, the more likely it is that a company car will be tax efficient.

*14 – Total Mileage in Each Tax Year*
Determines non-business mileage and the reimbursement necessary to avoid a fuel benefit charge.

*15 – Business Mileage in each Tax Year*
Determines the tax free value of fuel or mileage claims and capital allowances for the self-employed.

*16 – Availability for Private Use*
Can minimise or remove the tax liability on a company car.

*17 – Advisory Fuel Rates*
Determines the tax-free value of fuel claims by employees with company cars.

*18 – Approved Mileage Rates*
Determines the tax-free value of mileage for the self-employed.

*19 – Engine Size (Cylinder Capacity)*
Determines the advisory fuel rates applicable to company cars.

*20 – Re-sale Value*
Determines the written-down value of the main rate or special rate pools for capital allowances.

*21 – Period of Ownership*
Determines the total costs of the car over the time it is used.

*22 – Your Marginal Tax Rate*
Determines the tax payable on a company car or the tax saved by the self-employed.

*23 – Class 1A National Insurance Rate*
Determines the employer national insurance payable on a company car.

*24 – Class 4 National Insurance Rate*
Determines the national insurance on profits that can be saved by the self-employed.

*25 – Your Company's Marginal Tax Rate*
Determines the corporation tax saved on a company car and/or business mileage.

*26 – VAT Fuel Scale Charges*
Determines the output tax payable on fuel for a company car.

*27 – VAT Standard Rate*
Determines the input tax recoverable on lease rentals, fuel costs and other running costs. Also affects capital allowances and the list price of company cars.

There is one other factor that will influence you in these decisions and that is your very own cost of capital.


## The Cost of Capital

First of all, what do we mean by the economic expression *cost of capital*. And why should we have to start contemplating esoteric concepts like opportunity cost and net present value when all we are trying to do is decide whether to have a company car or not?

Well, it's because each individual (or company) has their own personal cost of capital, and I'm not just talking about the interest rate charged by your bank or finance company.

For example, if you want to buy a car in your own name rather than that of your company to avoid the dreaded car benefit tax rules, you will have to pay for it yourself. That will mean either borrowing the money to buy it from an external lender or diverting cash from your own financial resources, which you might have had other plans for.

In either case there will be a cost of capital, which will be either the interest charged by the lender or the opportunity cost of not investing the funds elsewhere.

True, you could borrow the money from your company or take a higher bonus or dividend to pay for it instead, but as we shall discover there are adverse tax consequences in doing this.

In any case, the company will have its own cost of capital and there may well be other plans for that cash which will compete with your desire to buy a new car.

We will return to the subject of finance costs in the case studies below. As we shall see, they can make a crucial difference to your decision.

## The 10 Key Decisions

There are 10 key decisions that affect people using their cars for work.

The ones you have to address depend on whether you are a business owner or a regular employee.

And if you are a business owner, it will depend on whether you trade through a limited company or not.

Whichever group you belong to, you should only need to consider around 4-5 of these questions. For simplicity, I have listed the first 6 decisions under Business Owners and the other 4 under Regular Employees.

## Business Owners

1) If you work through a limited company, should you have a company car or own it in your own name?

2) If you are a sole trader or partnership, should you claim business mileage or capital allowances/running costs?

3) If you work through a company, should you pay for fuel yourself or get the company to pay for it?

4) Which method should you use for claiming back VAT on fuel costs?

5) Should you purchase the car outright or lease it for a fixed term?

6) What type of car should you buy or lease?

## Regular Employees

7) Should you have a company car or a cash alternative?

8) Should you enter into a salary sacrifice arrangement for a company car?

9) Should you pay for fuel yourself or allow the company to pay for it?

10) If you do have a company car, which type of car should you have?

Each of these key decisions will now be explored at length and, where applicable, illustrated with case studies and tables.

# Chapter 8

# Decision # 1
# Company Car or Own Car?

## Relevant Factors

Probably the biggest decision a business owner has to make is whether to go the company car route or own the car personally.

A limited company is a legal entity separate from those who own or manage it, and is able to own property, such as cars and vans.

Of course, this decision is only relevant to those who run their own limited companies. It is not relevant to sole traders or partners as their cars will always be in their own name.

The main factors you need to consider are as follows:

- Finance costs
- Tax consequences
- Capital allowances
- Fuel costs
- Running costs
- Business mileage

## Finance Costs

There will always be some kind of finance cost because both you and the company have a cost of capital, and this will relate to either external borrowing costs or internal opportunity costs. There are always alternative ways of spending money, and this goes for the company as well as you.

Suppose you decide to buy a car in your own name and borrow the money to pay for it. The finance company charges you interest at 10% per annum. Let's assume that 10% is your cost of capital. The total finance cost over the lifetime of the car will be a negative factor when weighing up the advantages and disadvantages of owning it yourself.

Alternatively, you could get the company to pay for the car out of surplus funds, but those surplus funds have other potential uses too, even if they are just lying around in a bank account earning some interest.

On the other hand, the company might need those funds to avoid overdraft charges, or to pay for much needed plant and equipment, which it would otherwise need to borrow money to buy.

Without those funds, it might be necessary to discount its invoices to encourage customers to pay early and thus ensure it has adequate cash flow to meet its immediate liabilities. The opportunity cost would then be much higher.

Whatever the opportunity cost happens to be, it will be a negative factor when weighing up the advantages and disadvantages of using company funds to buy a car and should be brought into the equation alongside your own finance cost.

Let's consider another scenario. You can afford to buy the car yourself from your savings but choose to let the company pay for it instead. The company has more than enough working capital for its needs, has nothing else to spend the money on and no inclination to invest it elsewhere.

The company uses funds in a deposit account earning 2.5% per annum to buy the car. We can assume that 2.5% is its cost of capital.

If you spend your own money instead, you will also lose interest. Your own cost of capital will therefore be similar to that of the company and the finance cost will make little difference to your decision either way.

On the other hand, you might have been planning to start another business with that money or invest it in shares. Perhaps you could have expected a 5% rate of return but decided to spend it on a car instead. Now your cost of capital is double that of the company. In this situation, using your own funds is more expensive than using the company's.

I explained above that you need to take the tax effects into account too. Most of these are explained under the *Tax and National Insurance* heading, but there are some tax effects that are worth mentioning separately. If you borrow money from your company, there are two tax implications you need to consider:

- Income tax and Class IA national insurance on a beneficial loan
- Corporation tax on a participator loan

### *Beneficial Loans*

All loans to directors and employees above £5,000 are potential benefits in kind, even if the balance owing on that loan (or loans) only exceeded £5,000 for one day during the tax year.

In practice you would not be taxed on a loan if it existed for less than a month (calculated from the 6th day of one month to the 5th day of the next) because the taxable value of such loans tends to be worked out on an averaging basis. Under this method, the loan is taxed according to the number of complete months during which the loan was outstanding. However, the taxman does have the option of substituting a more precise calculation based on the number of days if it appears that the normal method produces a perverse result (as far as the taxman is concerned, that is).

The taxable value of loans from your employer is based on the *official rate of interest*. This rate is normally reviewed once a year by the taxman, although it is changed more frequently if base rates are not stable. At present the official rate is 4% and has been so since 6th April 2010.

If your loan is tax free the taxable value of the loan will be based on that rate. If you pay the company interest on the loan but below the official rate, you will be taxed on the difference. The employer will also have to pay Class 1A national insurance on the taxable value of the loan at 13.8%.

You could of course avoid any taxable benefit-in-kind by paying interest to the company at the official rate. If the company belongs to you, then you are effectively paying yourself interest so in that sense it has no financial effect.

However, the company will have to pay corporation tax on the interest received from you. For small companies this will be at 20%. You may also wish to extract the money from the company again at some point in the future, which means that it will be taxed again.

## Participator Loans

All loans to 'participators' in a close company that are outstanding at the end of its financial year (and remain outstanding nine months later) incur a 25% tax charge.

This is added to the company's corporation tax bill and must be paid within nine months of the year end. Without digressing to explain the terms 'participator' and 'close company', suffice it to say that, if you run your own company, it means you!

Fortunately, tax on participator loans is repayable once the loan has been repaid. In that sense, the tax is more in the nature of a temporary bond. It is also refunded if repayment of the loan is waived or the loan is written off for some reason. However, the borrower would then be taxed on the amount waived or written off as if it was income, and the company will not get tax relief on the write-off if the loan was to a connected party.

You can avoid a participator loan by ensuring that any money borrowed from your company is repaid by the year end. If that fails, then make sure it is repaid within nine months. You would still have to declare it on your Corporation Tax return but at least you won't have to pay tax on it.

However, don't be tempted to cook up some scheme whereby the loan is repaid a few days before the year end and then drawn down again shortly afterwards. That would be construed as false accounting and you may end up being prosecuted for it, especially as the intention was to evade tax!

If you borrow money from your company to pay for a car it is unlikely to be repaid in such a short time unless it was meant to be a temporary bridging loan. Therefore, the 25% temporary tax charge may be unavoidable. Even though you get the money back later, it would of course have a detrimental effect on cash-flow which means that there will be a finance cost.

## Tax Consequences

Tax and national insurance can be quite steep on company cars and is a major deterrent to having one. Most people with limited companies are better off buying cars in their own name. Yet it is often not understood that buying a car with your own money, or borrowing from the company to buy a car, can also have adverse tax consequences and these must be brought into the equation too.

### Tax Implications of a Company Car

Firstly, let us remind ourselves how tax on company cars is assessed. The basic calculation is as follows:

*List Price x Appropriate Percentage x Marginal Tax Rate*

The appropriate percentage is based on fuel type and $CO_2$ emissions. It can be anywhere between zero and 35% depending on how green your car is, and I'm not talking about the colour of the paintwork!

Yes, I did say zero! That is because some company cars are tax free, courtesy of a Government incentive that came in on 6th April 2010. For five years from that date, all cars that are incapable of producing any $CO_2$ emissions at all enjoy a 0% benefit-in-kind tax charge. Of course, in practice, that means electric cars.

Cars with $CO_2$ emissions between 1 and 75 g/km will only have a 5% benefit-in-kind charge for the 2 years ending 6th April 2012. Unfortunately, at the time of writing, there do not appear to be any cars on the market yet with $CO_2$ emissions in that range, so at present this rule is more or less irrelevant.

For all other cars the benefit-in-kind charge currently starts at 10% of list price for cars with $CO_2$ emissions up to 120 g/km (plus 3% for diesels) in the 2010/11 tax year. Above that the rate jumps to 15% for cars in the range 121-129 g/km.

From 6th April 2012 the 10% rate only applies to petrol-fuelled cars with $CO_2$ emissions up to 99 g/km. For cars above that threshold the rate will rise by 1% for every 5% increase in $CO_2$ emissions. For diesels obviously the minimum rate will be 13%.

## Tax Implications of Buying a Car Yourself

If you buy the car personally from your own financial resources then obviously you escape tax on a company car but you may need to take a higher salary or dividend from the company in order to finance the purchase.

If you are already a higher-rate taxpayer, taking a dividend will effectively cost you 25% of the cash received from the company. If you are an additional rate taxpayer (ie you earn more than £150,000 per annum) taking a dividend will cost you 36.1%.

Dividends are paid without deduction of tax, so if you require £21,000 to buy a new car and you are a higher-rate taxpayer you will need to declare a dividend of £28,000 in order to cover the tax bill. That is the net cash dividend, not the grossed-up dividend (including the notional tax credit) that goes on your tax return. However, there is no national insurance on dividends so you only have income tax to worry about.

25% may not sound too bad for tax on dividends, but bear in mind that the company must pay corporation tax on the profits those dividends come out of at anything between 20% and 27.5% (2011/12 rates).

So dividends can get quite expensive once you go above the higher-rate tax threshold. That threshold is £35,000 for 2011/12 by the way, and after adding £7,475 for your personal allowance it means that you can only earn £42,475 before dividends become liable to income tax.

Alternatively you could vote yourself a bonus or a pay rise instead. This will be subject to income tax and national insurance. For example, if you are already a higher-rate taxpayer and want £21,000 to buy a new car, you will need a bonus of £36,207 in 2011/12 (assuming tax and NI of 42% at marginal rates).

On the plus side, the company can claim payroll costs against corporation tax so you might think that you are better off taking bonus or salary rather than dividend. Not so unfortunately. Most owner-managers only take a notional salary from their companies to keep their national insurance contributions down (or at least those with good accountants do) and take the bulk of their remuneration as dividends.

If you then take a large bonus on top of that to buy a car, all you will succeed in doing is shunting your dividends into the higher-rate tax bracket, as salary and bonuses come before dividends in the queue to be taxed. Not only will you pay tax on the bonus but you may also end up paying tax on a dividend that would otherwise have been tax free.

You must also consider national insurance contributions. Employees pay 12% on earned income up to the Upper Earnings Threshold (£42,475 in 2011/12) and 2% above that.

However, the company pays 13.8% in employer contributions on top of this, and there is no cap on earnings subject to employer national insurance, so overall you could fork out up to 65.8% in PAYE on a bonus (being 50% tax + 2% employee national insurance + 13.8% employer national insurance).

The only silver lining is that the employer national insurance is a tax deductible expense for the company, so if corporation tax is 20% the net cost of employer NI is 13.8% x 80% = 11.04%.

So how about borrowing the money from your company instead? Could this save you any tax? Maybe yes, in the short term. However, unless you pay the company interest, it will be taxed as a beneficial loan and also probably as a participator loan (see above). Plus of course, you will have to pay the loan back one day.

Sometimes, however, there is merit in a participator loan. They are usually best avoided, but if you are thinking of closing your company down in the next few years, it would be perverse to pay higher-rate tax on dividends when you could take a loan instead and ultimately pay just 10% capital gains tax on the retained profits after re-paying the loan and claiming Entrepreneurs Relief.

From the above, you will see that very careful tax planning is required if you wish to take a bonus or dividend to subsidise a new car. Higher rates of income tax and national insurance coupled with lower rates of corporation tax are shifting the goalposts a bit. You may well find that in certain situations you are better off with a company car instead.

# Capital Allowances

The next plank in our analysis is capital allowances. These are only available if you go down the company car route. If you work through your own limited company but decide to keep the car in your own name, you cannot claim capital allowances for it. This contrasts with the position for owners of unincorporated businesses such as sole traders and partnerships who *can* claim capital allowances on their cars.

So the key question here is whether it is worth having a company car just to claim capital allowances. In fact, this is one of the major factors affecting your decision whether to put the car in your own name or that of your company:

- **If you have a company car you can claim capital allowances but will pay income tax and employer national insurance on a benefit-in-kind.**

- **If you keep the car in your own name, you avoid tax on a car benefit but cannot claim capital allowances.**

Obviously it depends on how much the capital allowances are worth. The magic numbers are 110 g/km and 160 g/km:

- If $CO_2$ emissions are 110 g/km or less you can claim a 100% capital allowance.

- If they are above 160 g/km you can only claim 10% per year on a reducing balance basis (8% from 1st April 2012).

- In between you can claim 20% per annum, again on a reducing balance basis (18% from 1st April 2012).

The table below illustrates the value of capital allowances against the tax and national insurance cost over a five year time frame for a new car costing £25,000.

To keep this simple, I have assumed that the list price is also £25,000. The list price is not usually the same as the purchase price for new cars but the difference is not generally high enough on new cars to distort the calculations much.

The resale value is also important when it comes to calculating the value of capital allowances. The higher the resale value the lower your capital allowances will be but you will recover your net capital cost more quickly.

A simple example will illustrate this principle.

Suppose you buy a car with $CO_2$ emissions of 140 g/km for £25,000 in April 2011 and sell it in April 2015 for £8,000. This means the net cost of the car is £17,000. Capital allowances would be as follows:

| Tax Year | WDA Rate | Capital Allowance | Disposal proceeds | Pool Value c/f | Total Claimed | Net Cost | Proportion Claimed |
|---|---|---|---|---|---|---|---|
| 2011/12 | 20% | £5,000 | | £20,000 | £5,000 | | |
| 2012/13 | 18% | £3,600 | | £16,400 | £8,600 | | |
| 2013/14 | 18% | £2,952 | | £13,448 | £11,552 | | |
| 2014/15 | 18% | £2,421 | £8,000 | £3,027 | £13,973 | £17,000 | 82.2% |
| 2015/16 | 18% | £545 | | £2,482 | £14,518 | £17,000 | 85.4% |

**Note**
* WDA stands for writing-down allowance
* The £8,000 disposal proceeds are subtracted from the pool value carried forward

You can see from this table that the company will claim tax relief on just 85% of the net cost of the car by the disposal date.

Once the pool value carried forward is less than £1,000 it can be written off immediately and claimed on the next company tax return. However, this is unlikely to happen if new items are constantly added to the pool.

Now let's see what the figures look like if the company sells the car for £10,000 instead.

| Tax Year | WDA Rate | Capital Allowance | Disposal Proceeds | Pool Value c/f | Total Claimed | Net Cost | Proportion Claimed |
|---|---|---|---|---|---|---|---|
| 2011/12 | 20% | £5,000 | | £20,000 | £5,000 | | |
| 2012/13 | 18% | £3,600 | | £16,400 | £8,600 | | |
| 2013/14 | 18% | £2,952 | | £13,448 | £11,552 | | |
| 2014/15 | 18% | £2,421 | £10,000 | £1,027 | £13,973 | £15,000 | 93.2% |
| 2015/16 | 18% | £185 | | £842 | £14,158 | £15,000 | 94.4% |

The percentages in the last column are significantly higher. The higher resale value enables the company to recover its net capital cost far more quickly, even though capital allowances are lower.

Company cars that hold their values well are therefore more tax-efficient than those that depreciate fairly quickly, particularly now that companies cannot claim balancing allowances on cars bought since 1st April 2009 (balancing allowances are catch-up tax deductions that make up for any shortfall in tax relief when the car is sold.)

On the other side of the coin, a car with a high resale value may be more tax efficient to keep in your own name, as you can keep the sale proceeds yourself. Therefore, you may be able to survive on a lower dividend in the year of sale and save income tax.

The other major factor to take into account on capital allowances is any large discrepancy between the purchase price of the car and the manufacturer's list price.

Income tax on company cars is based on the list price, capital allowances on the actual purchase price.

Therefore, tax on the car benefit-in-kind will tend to outweigh capital allowances more and more on second-hand cars. A company car is far more likely to be beneficial from a tax point of view if it is a brand new car.

## Fuel Costs

Fuel costs are normally a minor factor when deciding whether to have a company car or not because most company car owners pay for their own fuel anyway.

However, fuel costs could still influence the decision in another way. On a company car, your company must reimburse you for business mileage according to the latest advisory fuel rates.

For a diesel car up to 2000cc this is currently 15p per mile. These rates will be tax free for you and the company can claim the cost against corporation tax.

On the other hand, if the car is in your own name, the company can reimburse you for business mileage at the approved mileage rates, which are now 45p per mile for the first 10,000 miles per tax year and 25p thereafter. Again, this will be tax free for you and the company can claim the cost against corporation tax.

However, because the advisory fuel rates are regularly updated in line with prices at the pumps, whereas the approved mileage rates tend to remain frozen for many years, the advisory fuel rates are gradually catching up with the approved mileage rates.

The mileage rates may still look generous (45p per mile) but they do not cover just fuel. They are meant to compensate the owner of the car for other running costs plus capital allowances.

Therefore, if fuel prices continue to rise, the tax-free mileage rates will become gradually less attractive and make it less tax efficient to keep the car in your own name.

Fuel consumption also plays a part here. If you have a gas guzzler that needs filling up every time you run the kids to school, you may be able to convince the taxman that the advisory fuel rates are too low in your case and obtain permission to claim more.

This will reduce the attractiveness of the mileage rates which are fixed no matter how much you personally spend on fuel. On the other hand, if you are a tree hugger and have a car that does about 100 miles to the gallon, you will probably benefit more from the mileage rates.

## Running Costs

Insurance, road tax, maintenance bills, accident repairs, breakdown recovery, lease rentals and most other costs associated with a car can be paid by the company if it owns the vehicle.

There is no benefit-in-kind income tax charge payable by the employee in respect of these costs. Furthermore, they are fully deductible for corporation tax purposes.

Not so if you own the vehicle personally. Then you have to pay these bills out of your own pocket and the company cannot claim them against tax.

Obviously this is a major consideration for an ordinary employee who does not own the company he works for. Having your employer pay for the running costs is a huge benefit which goes some way towards mitigating the tax bill on a company car.

However, if you own the company, it may not make too much difference. After all, you own the company and its cash is essentially your cash, so what benefit is there in getting the company to pay the running costs?

Well as it happens there are two benefits. Firstly, it's a good way to extract cash from the company. If you pay yourself extra salary or dividends to cover your motoring costs there could be income tax and possibly national insurance to pay on these amounts.

Secondly, the company can claim the bills against corporation tax and also claim back any VAT on them (if it is VAT registered) as they are costs associated with maintaining a company asset.

To sum up, running costs will only be a major factor in your decision if you own a very high-maintenance car. Even then, they are only likely to sway the decision in a borderline case where the other factors more or less offset each other. However, over a period of four years or more, they could make quite a big difference.

## Business Use

It may seem odd, but it is sometimes best to keep a car with high levels of business use in your own name rather than that of the company. That may strike you as counter-intuitive.

To understand this anomaly, we have to go back to the tax-free mileage rates (45p per mile for the first 10,000 miles; 25p thereafter; 5p extra for passengers).

If you do a lot of business mileage in your car you could receive a significant tax-free payment from your company.

Someone driving 10,000 miles can claim £4,500 tax free. Someone driving 18,000 miles can claim £6,500 tax free. Your company can claim these amounts against corporation tax, so at the 20% corporation tax rate you could get the taxman to pay £1,300 for 18,000 miles.

This is a lot more than can be claimed with the current advisory fuel rates, although the 45p mileage rate is meant to cover ALL running costs, so they're not strictly comparable.

To obtain a true comparison you would need to factor in the other running costs and capital allowances too.

Whoever owns the car, you can always get your company to pay for motoring costs directly related to that business journey, such as parking fees, road tolls and congestion charges, so these items are always neutral in deciding whether to have a company car or not.

In practice, the amount of business use will rarely decide the issue on its own. If it is worth having a company car after weighing up all the other factors, it would probably still be worth having one even if the car does have a lot of business use.

Similarly, if it is worth keeping a car in your own name, low business use will not make you change your mind. Nonetheless, it is a relevant factor to enter into the mix and the case studies below will illustrate the effect it has on the overall decision.

## Multiple Owner Companies

Before proceeding with the case studies, it is worth mentioning that these only apply to companies owned by one individual, or by married couples, civil partners, co-habitees, families, etc.

If people from different households own shares in the company, then the comparisons will not work because not all the cash flows can be attributed to you or your family.

For example, if you own a company along with two other directors and buy yourself a company car, they would probably have something to say about it unless they had a car too (or a benefit of equivalent value).

Even if you did all have company cars, they are likely to have different taxable values. With a husband and wife company this is less likely to be an issue because your spouse will probably benefit from the car as much as you.

It is still possible to use these guidelines for companies in which you only own some of the shares, but remember that it is not always a simple matter of taking a straight percentage of the company cash flows, and the decision may not be just yours to make anyway.

## Case Studies 1.1 to 1.6 – Dirty Car

There now follows a series of case studies illustrating how all these factors come together in practice. These focus on the *relevant* cash flows in each case, ignoring those factors that are neutral in the final decision, and arrive at a bottom line value either for or against a company car.

They cannot possibly cover all possible scenarios, otherwise we would have to do thousands of them, but they can be used as a template for creating your own model to suit your own individual circumstances.

The first group of case studies looks at a particularly 'dirty' car with high levels of $CO_2$ emissions. Not surprisingly the outcome is generally against taking a company car in these examples, at least as far as owner-managers are concerned.

The second group of case studies looks at the greener alternative and measures the extent to which a company car would be tax-efficient. The case studies show that company owners should sometimes consider taking a company car if the car has low $CO_2$ emissions.

The third batch of case studies attempts to identify the point at which company cars become viable by tweaking the various factors involved. This will differ according to the factor tweaked.

### *Important Assumptions*

One thing you should bear in mind when looking at these case studies is that I have used the 2012/13 car benefit percentages for all future tax years, even though these will increase.

I have also used the latest advisory fuel rates at the time of writing (effective 1st September 2011) for future tax years, even though it is likely these will change in line with prices at the pumps.

Neither assumption should affect the overall outcome.

## Case Study # 1.1 – High Business Mileage

Dirty Den bought an 1800cc petrol-fuelled car on 6$^{th}$ April 2011 with a list price of £25,000 and $CO_2$ emissions of 180 g/km. This means the car has a benefit in kind charge of 26%/27% over the period.

He pays for all fuel himself and drives 20,000 miles a year with fuel costs of 18p per mile.

He claims 15,000 business miles a year at the maximum tax-free rates, incurs other running costs of £2,000 a year (of which £1,000 includes VAT) and expects to sell the car exactly 4 years later for £8,000.

The car will cost £24,000 and he can either get his own company, Beastenders Ltd, to buy it as a company car or he can declare a dividend of £24,000 and use the money to buy the car himself.

Beastenders Ltd earns 2.5% interest per annum on its cash and Den earns 3% per annum on his own savings. Cost of capital is only relevant for the time the car is owned and applies only to the purchase cost and sale proceeds. It is nil on all other cash flows.

Den pays income tax at 25% on cash dividends and 40% on the car benefit. Beastenders Ltd pays corporation tax at 20%.

Den will reduce his dividend by £8,000 in Year 4 if the car is in his name (he will receive £8,000 in sales proceeds from the car so doesn't need as much dividend income).

Beastenders Ltd will ultimately claim the whole capital allowance if it is a company car.

What is the most tax efficient option?

| Company Car | |
|---|---|
| Income tax on benefit in kind<br>£25,000 x 26%/27% x 4 years x 40% tax | +£10,700 |
| Employer national insurance on benefit in kind<br>£25,000 x 26%/27% x 4 years x 13.8% | +£3,692 |
| Less: Corporation tax saved on employer NI<br>£3,692 x 20% | -£738 |
| Less: Capital allowances<br>£24,000 - £8,000 x 20% corporation tax | -£3,200 |
| Less: Corporation tax saved on fuel<br>15,000 miles x 18p x 4 years x 20% corporation tax | -£2,160 |
| Less: Corporation tax saved on running costs<br>£2,000 - £167 VAT x 4 years x 20% | -£1,466 |
| Less: VAT saved on running costs<br>£1,000 x 4 years x 20/120 | -£667 |
| **Relevant cash flows** | **+£6,161** |
| | |
| **Own Car** | |
| Income tax on net dividend in Year 1<br>£24,000 x 25% | +£6,000 |
| Less: Income tax saved on net dividend in Year 4<br>£8,000 x 25% | -£2,000 |
| Less: Corporation tax saved, first 10,000 miles<br>10,000 x 45p x 4 years x 20% | -£3,600 |
| Less: Corporation tax saved, next 5,000 miles<br>5,000 x 25p x 4 years x 20% | -£1,000 |
| **Relevant cash flows** | **-£600** |
| | |
| **Additional cost of company car** | **+£6,761** |

This example produces the usual result. Company cars are much more expensive, in this example £6,761 more expensive!

Note here that we only need to compare *relevant* cash flows. In practice, this means just the *tax* effects of the various cash flows. All neutral costs are taken out of the equation.

As Den owns his company, we can assume that the costs of a company car are ultimately borne by him. In that sense, it doesn't matter whether it is him or the company that pays for the car and its running costs. Therefore, the purchase price, sale proceeds, fuel and running costs are irrelevant to the decision.

The cost of capital is also irrelevant in this example as company deposits are used to fund the purchase of the car in either case, either directly or via a dividend.

Likewise, the sale proceeds will come back to the company at the end of Year 4, either directly or because Den takes a lower dividend that year. Den has no finance cost over the four years as the cost of capital is nil on the running costs (in reality this is very unlikely but it is not material enough to affect the decision).

VAT has been brought into the equation because the company can recover input tax on maintenance bills (assuming it is VAT registered and does not use the flat rate scheme) whilst Den cannot recover VAT if the car is owned by him personally.

The company can also claim all running costs against corporation (after deducting input tax).

This example has been simplified in the sense that tax rates are assumed to remain unchanged from April 2011 onwards and we have completely ignored the time value of money.

In particular, it would take the company 20 years to claim 90% of the capital allowance (at 10% going down to 8% per annum on a reducing balance basis after adding back the sale proceeds in Year 4). However, neither of these factors would make much difference in this example.

We can assume that, in most cases where $CO_2$ levels are fairly high, the outcome shown above would be the default position.

In this situation, it is almost always better for owner managers to buy the car in their own name rather than have a company car.

Nonetheless, we will now test various other scenarios to see whether there are any circumstances in which a company car would be better with these $CO_2$ emissions.

## Case Study # 1.2 – High Running Costs

Let us assume that the car is very high maintenance. Fuel consumption is only 20 miles to the gallon, garage bills are extortionate (he has it serviced by a main dealer) and it belongs to a very high insurance group. Running costs are £4,000 per annum (of which £2,000 includes VAT) and fuel costs are 25p per mile. How much difference does this make?

| Company Car | |
|---|---|
| Income tax on benefit in kind<br>£25,000 x 26%/27% x 4 years x 40% tax | +£10,700 |
| Employer national insurance on benefit in kind<br>£25,000 x 26%/27% x 4 years x 13.8% | +£3,692 |
| Less: Corporation tax saved on employer NI<br>£3,692 x 20% | -£738 |
| Less: Capital allowances<br>£24,000 - £8,000 x 20% corporation tax | -£3,200 |
| Less: Corporation tax saved on fuel<br>15,000 miles x 25p x 4 years x 20% | -£3,000 |
| Less: Corporation tax saved on running costs<br>£4,000 - £333 VAT x 4 years x 20% | -£2,934 |
| Less: VAT saved on running costs<br>£2,000 x 4 years x 20/120 | -£1,333 |
| **Relevant cash flows** | **+£3,187** |
| | |
| **Own Car** | |
| Income tax on net dividend in Year 1<br>£24,000 x 25% | +£6,000 |
| Less: Income tax saved on net dividend in Year 4<br>£8,000 x 25% | -£2,000 |
| Less: Corporation tax saved on first 10,000 miles<br>10,000 x 45p x 4 years x 20% | -£3,600 |
| Less: Corporation tax saved on next 5,000 miles<br>5,000 x 25p x 4 years x 20% | -£1,000 |
| **Relevant cash flows** | **-£600** |
| | |
| **Additional cost of company car** | **+£3,787** |

We have assumed here that Den made out a very good case for not sticking to the advisory fuel rates and the taxman believed him (not so easy in practice). It is very unlikely that the taxman would have allowed him to claim 25p instead of 15p, but we shall suspend reality for a moment here to see what sort of effect that would have on the figures.

Obviously the relevant cash flows on the Own Car side of the equation do not change as Den can still only claim the approved mileage rates (45p and 25p) and cannot save tax on the running costs. However, on the Company Car side of the equation Den can save extra corporation tax of £3,334.

The company car still costs £3,787 more than a car in his own name. The gap has narrowed significantly but still not enough to sway the decision.

## Case Study # 1.3 – Low Business Mileage

Maybe the amount of business use will tilt the balance in favour of a company car. I have already suggested that low levels of business use may make a company car more attractive. Let's see if that is true. Suppose Den only drives 5,000 business miles a year. How will this affect the tax savings?

| Company Car | |
|---|---|
| Income tax on benefit in kind<br>£25,000 x 26%/27% x 4 years x 40% tax | -£10,700 |
| Employer national insurance on benefit in kind<br>£25,000 x 26%/27% x 4 years x 13.8% | +£3,692 |
| Less: Corporation tax saved on employer NI<br>£3,692 x 20% | -£738 |
| Less: Capital allowances<br>£24,000 - £8,000 x 20% corporation tax | -£3,200 |
| Less: Corporation tax saved on fuel<br>5,000 miles x 25p x 4 years x 20% | -£1,000 |
| Less: Corporation tax saved on running costs<br>£4,000 - £333 x 4 years x 20% | -£2,934 |
| Less: VAT saved on running costs<br>£2,000 x 4 years x 20/120 | -£1,333 |
| **Relevant cash flows** | **+£5,187** |
| | |
| **Own Car** | |
| Income tax on net dividend in Year 1<br>£24,000 x 25% | +£6,000 |
| Less: Income tax saved on net dividend in Year 4<br>£8,000 x 25% | -£2,000 |
| Less: Corporation tax saved on 5,000 miles<br>5,000 x 45p x 4 years x 20% | -£1,800 |
| **Relevant cash flows** | **+£2,200** |
| | |
| **Additional cost of company car** | **+£2,987** |

The net differential only changes by £800 so it still doesn't close the gap. The company car still costs more by £2,987.

## Case Study # 1.4 – Basic-rate Taxpayer

So far all these examples have assumed that Den is a higher-rate taxpayer, but suppose he reduces his income so that, even with a company car, his taxable income is below the higher-rate threshold. To compare like with like, we need to assume that he would also be below the higher-rate threshold if he buys the car in his own name and takes a dividend to pay for it. The next example uses the same data as Case Study # 1.3 but assumes that Den pays tax only at the basic-rate.

| Company Car | |
|---|---|
| Income tax on benefit in kind<br>£25,000 x 26%/27% x 4 years x 20% income tax | +£5,350 |
| Employer national insurance on benefit in kind<br>£25,000 x 26%/27% x 4 years x 13.8% | +£3,692 |
| Less: Corporation tax saved on employer NI<br>£3,692 x 20% | -£738 |
| Less: Capital allowances<br>£24,000 - £8,000 x 20% corporation tax | -£3,200 |
| Less: Corporation tax saved on fuel<br>5,000 miles x 25p x 4 years x 20% corporation tax | -£1,000 |
| Less: Corporation tax saved on running costs<br>£4,000-£333 x 4 years x 20% corporation tax | -£2,934 |
| Less: VAT saved on running costs<br>£2,000 x 4 years x 20/120 | -£1,333 |
| **Relevant cash flows** | **-£163** |
| | |
| **Own Car** | |
| Income tax on net dividend in Year 1<br>£24,000 x 0% | +£0 |
| Less: Income tax saved on net dividend in Year 4<br>£8,000 x 0% | -£0 |
| Less: Corporation tax saved on 5,000 miles<br>5,000 x 45p x 4 years x 20% | -£1,800 |
| **Relevant cash flows** | **-£1,800** |
| | |
| **Additional cost of company car** | **+£1,637** |

This is a closer result than Case Study # 1.3 but a company car is still far more expensive, even though the tax on the benefit is halved. That is because there is no longer any tax on the dividend if Den keeps his income below the higher-rate threshold.

## Case Study # 1.5 – Higher Corporation Tax

The fact that Beastenders Ltd only saves tax at 20% whereas Den pays tax at 40% on a company car obviously makes a big difference. Suppose the company makes profits of more than £300,000. Its marginal rate of tax would be 27.5% in 2011/12. We'll assume the same data as Case Study # 1.3 over a four year time frame. Let's see how this affects the decision.

| Company Car | |
|---|---|
| Income tax on benefit in kind £25,000 x 26%/27% x 4 years x 40% tax | +£10,700 |
| Employer national insurance on benefit in kind £25,000 x 26%/27% x 4 years x 13.8% | +£3,692 |
| Less: Corporation tax saved on employer NI £3,692 x 27.5% | -£1,015 |
| Less: Capital allowances £24,000 - £8,000 x 27.5% corporation tax | -£4,400 |
| Less: Corporation tax saved on fuel 5,000 miles x 25p x 4 years x 27.5% corporation tax | -£1,375 |
| Less: Corporation tax saved on running costs £4,000 - £333 x 4 years x 27.5% corporation tax | -£4,034 |
| Less: VAT saved on running costs £2,000 x 4 years x 20/120 | -£1,333 |
| **Relevant cash flows** | **+£2,235** |
| | |
| **Own Car** | |
| Income tax on net dividend in Year 1 £24,000 x 25% | +£6,000 |
| Less: Income tax saved on net dividend in Year 4 £8,000 x 25% | -£2,000 |
| Less: Corporation tax saved on 5,000 miles 5,000 x 45p x 4 years x 27.5% corporation tax | -£2,475 |
| **Relevant cash flows** | **+£1,525** |
| | |
| **Additional cost of company car** | **+£710** |

Saving tax at 27.5% instead of 20% clearly makes a huge difference, but not enough to sway the decision.

A company car is still marginally more expensive at 180 g/km, and one must also take into account the long delay in realising the full benefit of the capital allowances.

In fact, corporation tax rates for companies making profits above £300,000 will be coming down at 1% per annum until they reach 23% in April 2014.

This example does not reflect the gradual reduction in the marginal rate over the 4 years, so the additional cost of a company car would be much higher. However, it does not affect the overall conclusion.

### Case Study # 1.6 – Finance Costs

So far we haven't examined the effect of finance costs on the decision.

In the previous examples these were neutral because, in both cases, the cash to pay for the car was coming out of the company. But let's suppose there is a big differential in the cost of capital.

Let's assume the same data as Case Study # 1.1 but with one difference. Instead of taking a dividend from his company to pay for the car, Den has to use his own savings (perhaps because there are insufficient profits to declare a dividend).

He could have invested that cash in another venture that would have earned him an annual return of 10% over the 4 years he owns the car (but nothing after that and no compound interest, just to keep it simple).

Likewise, the company will only earn 2.5% on its money for 4 years (again, nothing after that and no compound interest).

Which is better now: a company car or own car?

| Company Car | |
|---|---:|
| Income tax on benefit in kind<br>£25,000 x 26%/27% x 4 years x 40% tax | +£10,700 |
| Employer national insurance on benefit in kind<br>£25,000 x 26%/27% x 4 years x 13.8% | +£3,692 |
| Less: Corporation tax saved on employer NI<br>£3,692 x 20% | -£738 |
| Less: Capital allowances<br>£24,000 - £8,000 x 20% corporation tax | -£3,200 |
| Less: Corporation tax saved on fuel<br>15,000 miles x 18p x 4 years x 20% | -£2,160 |
| Less: Corporation tax saved on running costs<br>£2,000 - £167 x 4 years x 20% | -£1,466 |
| Less: VAT saved on running costs<br>£1,000 x 4 years x 20/120 | -£667 |
| Finance cost<br>£24,000 x 2.5% x 4 years | +£2,400 |
| Less: Corporation tax saved on finance cost<br>£2,400 x 20% | -£480 |
| **Relevant cash flows** | **+£8,081** |
| | |
| **Own Car** | |
| Finance cost<br>£24,000 x 10% x 4 years | +£9,600 |
| Less: Income tax saved on finance cost<br>£9,600 x 40% | -£3,840 |
| Less: Corporation tax saved on first 10,000 miles<br>10,000 x 45p x 4 years x 20% | -£3,600 |
| Less: Corporation tax saved on next 5,000 miles<br>5,000 x 25p x 4 years x 20% | -£1,000 |
| | |
| **Relevant cash flows** | **+£1,160** |
| | |
| **Additional cost of company car** | **+£6,921** |

Clearly the finance costs are much higher for Den than for Beastenders Ltd. However, this is not enough to bridge the additional cost of a company car and in fact this widens by £160 to £6,921 because Den saves tax of £4,000 on the dividend. A company car would only be better for Den if his opportunity cost was say 18% per annum. Then the relevant cash flows for his own car would be £8,840 and a company car would be £759 cheaper. But of course, the huge length of time it takes to claim the capital allowances would then be far more relevant.

## Case Studies 2.1 to 2.6 – Green Car

From the examples so far, it would seem well nigh impossible for a company car with above average $CO_2$ levels to be more tax efficient than a car in your own name if the company happens to belong to you. The major factor is clearly the tax on company car users. It is so high in these examples that it trumps all other factors.

But suppose you chose a greener car instead. Rather than a gas guzzler churning out a filthy 180 g/km, suppose you buy a much smaller car with $CO_2$ emissions of just 109 g/km. In Jeremy Clarkson speak, a car your granny would be proud to drive!

### Case Study 2.1 – High Business Mileage

Mary Poppins buys a 1400cc petrol car on 6$^{th}$ April 2011 with a list price of £15,000 and $CO_2$ emissions of 109 g/km. She pays for all fuel herself and drives 20,000 miles a year with fuel costs of 10p per mile. She claims 15,000 business miles a year at the maximum tax-free rates, incurs other running costs of £2,000 a year (of which £1,000 includes VAT) and expects to sell the car exactly 4 years later for £3,000.

The car will cost £14,000 and she can either get her own company, Poppins Ltd (it's an umbrella company!) to buy it as a company car or she can declare a dividend of £14,000 and use that money to buy the car herself. Poppins Ltd earns 2.5% interest per annum on its cash and Mary earns 3% per annum on her own savings.

Mary pays income tax at 25% on net dividends and 40% on car benefit. Poppins Ltd pays corporation tax at 20%.

Mary will reduce her dividend by £3,000 in Year 4 if the car is in her name so her personal tax bill that year will decrease by 25% of that figure.

If it is a company car, Poppins Ltd will claim the whole purchase cost against tax in Year 1. This is due to the fact that $CO_2$ emissions do not exceed 110 g/km and the car therefore qualifies for an enhanced capital allowance of 100%.

Which is the most tax efficient option?

As with all the other case studies, it is only the tax effects we need to consider here as the underlying costs are neutral. She owns the company and its cash is essentially her cash, so at the end of the day it makes no difference whether she pays for the car herself or gets her company to pay for it. Finance costs are the same in both cases as the money to pay for the car is coming out of company funds, whether as a straight purchase or as a dividend to Mary. Likewise, the sale proceeds of £3,000 will eventually come back to the company, either directly or because Mary takes a lower dividend in Year 4.

| Company Car | |
| --- | --- |
| Income tax on benefit in kind<br>£15,000 x 10%/12% x 4 years x 40% tax | +£2,760 |
| Employer national insurance on benefit in kind<br>£15,000 x 10%/12% x 4 years x 13.8% | +£952 |
| Less: Corporation tax saved on employer NI<br>£952 x 20% | -£190 |
| Less: Capital allowances<br>£14,000 - £3,000 x 20% corporation tax | -£2,200 |
| Less: Corporation tax saved on fuel<br>15,000 miles x 15p x 4 years x 20% | -£1,800 |
| Less: Corporation tax saved on running costs<br>£2,000 - £167 x 4 years x 20% | -£1,466 |
| Less: VAT saved on running costs<br>£1,000 x 4 years x 20/120 | -£667 |
| **Relevant cash flows** | **-£2,611** |
|  |  |
| **Own Car** | |
| Income tax on net dividend in Year 1<br>£14,000 x 25% | +£3,500 |
| Less: Income tax saved on net dividend in Year 4<br>£3,000 x 25% | -£750 |
| Less: Corporation tax saved on first 10,000 miles<br>10,000 x 45p x 4 years x 20% | -£3,600 |
| Less: Corporation tax saved on next 5,000 miles<br>5,000 x 25p x 4 years x 20% | -£1,000 |
| **Relevant cash flows** | **-£1,850** |
|  |  |
| **Additional cost of company car** | **-£761** |

We can see in this case that it is £761 cheaper over the four years to have a company car.

That is probably just about enough to make it worthwhile going down the company car route.

Also, Poppins Ltd would get the full benefit of the capital allowance in the year of purchase as $CO_2$ emissions are not higher than 110 g/km – no 20 year wait for the capital allowances to fully materialise.

The tax advantage would be immediate. Admittedly, some of it would be clawed back in year four when the car is sold. Also, the company would not have to pay corporation tax until 9 months after its year end, so in that sense the capital allowance would still be delayed. Overall, however, the company would save £2,200 in tax on the net capital cost.

It is important to note that the special 10% income tax rate for cars with $CO_2$ emissions up to 120 g/km only applies until 5th April 2012. After that date, only company cars with $CO_2$ emissions up to 99 g/km will qualify for the 10% rate. At 100 g/km the tax rate will be 11% and it will then go up by 1% for each 5% increase in $CO_2$ emissions. Diesels will incur an additional 3%, as they do now.

However, on the plus side, it is possible that fuel prices (and hence the advisory fuel rates) will go up over the next few years whilst the tax free mileage rates will remain frozen. This may be enough to swing the decision more solidly in favour of the company car.

## Case Study 2.2 – Higher Corporation Tax Rates

Suppose Poppins Ltd had taxable profits of more than £300,000 and paid corporation tax at a marginal rate of 27.5%. Obviously this would make a company car more viable, but by how much?

| Company Car | |
|---|---|
| Income tax on benefit in kind<br>£15,000 x 10%/12% x 4 years x 40% tax | +£2,760 |
| Employer national insurance on benefit in kind<br>£15,000 x 10%/12% x 4 years x 13.8% | +£952 |
| Less: Corporation tax saved on employer NI<br>£952 x 27.5% | -£262 |
| Less: Capital allowances<br>£14,000 - £3,000 x 27.5% corporation tax | -£3,025 |
| Less: Corporation tax saved on fuel<br>15,000 miles x 15p x 4 years x 27.5% | -£2,475 |
| Less: Corporation tax saved on running costs<br>£2,000 - £167 x 4 years x 27.5% | -£2,016 |
| Less: VAT saved on running costs<br>£1,000 x 4 years x 20/120 | -£667 |
| **Relevant cash flows** | **-£4,733** |
| | |
| **Own Car** | |
| Income tax on net dividend in Year 1<br>£14,000 x 25% | +£3,500 |
| Less: Income tax saved on net dividend in Year 4<br>£3,000 x 25% | -£750 |
| Less: Corporation tax saved on first 10,000 miles<br>10,000 x 45p x 4 years x 27.5% corporation tax | -£4,950 |
| Less: Corporation tax saved on next 5,000 miles<br>5,000 x 25p x 4 years x 27.5% corporation tax | -£1,375 |
| **Relevant cash flows** | **-£3,575** |
| | |
| **Additional cost of company car** | **-£1,158** |

Perhaps not quite as much as we might have expected, as the company can claim back even more tax on the mileage rates if the car was in Mary's name than it could on the advisory fuel rates for a company car. If business use was lower, the effect would have been more pronounced.

Clearly company cars are more viable for larger businesses paying high marginal tax rates then they are for smaller ones paying just 20% corporation tax.

However, care needs to be taken with any calculations based on marginal corporation tax rates, as it is only the profits above the £300,000 mark that are effectively subject to these higher rates.

If profits are say £20,000 above the £300,000 mark, then having a company car may be sufficient to bring them below that threshold. In that case, you would need to calculate a hybrid tax rate and factor that into the equation instead.

It should also be noted that the above tax saving will be reduced from April 2012 as corporation tax rates continue to fall.

## Case Study 2.3 – Basic-rate Taxpayer

On the other side of the coin, perhaps Mary keeps her income below the higher-rate threshold and can avoid tax on the dividend necessary to buy the car. This would have a significant impact on the decision.

| Company Car | |
|---|---|
| Income tax on benefit in kind<br>£15,000 x 10%/12% x 4 years x 20% tax | +£1,380 |
| Employer national insurance on benefit in kind<br>£15,000 x 10%/12% x 4 years x 13.8% | +£952 |
| Less: Corporation tax saved on employer NI<br>£952 x 20% | -£190 |
| Less: Capital allowances<br>£14,000 - £3,000 x 20% corporation tax | -£2,200 |
| Less: Corporation tax saved on fuel<br>15,000 miles x 15p x 4 years x 20% | -£1,800 |
| Less: Corporation tax saved on running costs<br>£2,000 - £167 x 4 years x 20% | -£1,466 |
| Less: VAT saved on running costs<br>£1,000 x 4 years x 20/120 | -£667 |
| **Relevant cash flows** | **-£3,991** |
| | |
| **Own Car** | |
| Income tax on net dividend in Year 1<br>£14,000 x 0% | +£0 |
| Less: Income tax saved on net dividend in Year 4<br>£3,000 x 0% | -£0 |
| Less: Corporation tax saved on first 10,000 miles<br>10,000 x 45p x 4 years x 20% | -£3,600 |
| Less: Corporation tax saved on next 5,000 miles<br>5,000 x 25p x 4 years x 20% | -£1,000 |
| **Relevant cash flows** | **-£4,600** |
| | |
| **Additional cost of company car** | **+£609** |

Now, although tax on the benefit has been halved, the absence of tax on the dividend skews the calculation in favour of Mary buying the car in her own name. The most influential factor now is the corporation tax saved on business mileage. The differential of £2,800 between the mileage rates and the advisory fuel rate is sufficient now on its own to tilt the balance away from a company car.

### Case Study 2.4 – Lower Business Mileage

We will now examine what the outcome would be if business mileage was not so high. Suppose Mary only drives 5,000 miles a year on business. The following example uses the same data as Case Study # 2.3 but reduces business mileage from 15,000 to 5,000 per year.

| Company Car | |
|---|---:|
| Income tax on benefit in kind<br>£15,000 x 10%/12% x 4 years x 20% tax | +£1,380 |
| Employer national insurance on benefit in kind<br>£15,000 x 10%/12% x 4 years x 13.8% | +£952 |
| Less: Corporation tax saved on employer NI<br>£952 x 20% | -£190 |
| Less: Capital allowances<br>£14,000 - £3,000 x 20% corporation tax | -£2,200 |
| Less: Corporation tax saved on fuel<br>5,000 miles x 15p x 4 years x 20% | -£600 |
| Less: Corporation tax saved on running costs<br>£2,000 - £167 x 4 years x 20% | -£1,466 |
| Less: VAT saved on running costs<br>£1,000 x 4 years x 20/120 | -£667 |
| **Relevant cash flows** | **-£2,791** |
| | |
| **Own Car** | |
| Income tax on net dividend in Year 1<br>£14,000 x 0% | +£0 |
| Less: Income tax saved on net dividend in Year 4<br>£3,000 x 0% | -£0 |
| Less: Corporation tax saved on 5,000 miles<br>5,000 x 45p x 4 years x 20% | -£1,800 |
| **Relevant cash flows** | **-£1,800** |
| | |
| **Additional cost of company car** | **-£991** |

Now we are back in favour of a company car again. The net tax savings by the company are greater than the income tax charge on the company car. This proves that a company car may still be viable even if you are not a higher-rate taxpayer.

## Case Study 2.5 – Low Business Mileage, High Corporation Tax Rate

Now let's see what would happen if we combine low business mileage with a high corporation tax rate. Business mileage is just 5,000 miles per annum and the company pays tax at 27.5%. We will also assume that Mary is a higher-rate tax payer, which seems reasonable given that her company makes profits over £300,000.

| Company Car | |
|---|---|
| Income tax on benefit in kind<br>£15,000 x 10%/12% x 4 years x 40% tax | +£2,760 |
| Employer national insurance on benefit in kind<br>£15,000 x 10%/12% x 4 years x 13.8% | +£952 |
| Less: Corporation tax saved on employer NI<br>£952 x 27.5% | -£262 |
| Less: Capital allowances<br>£14,000 - £3,000 x 27.5% corporation tax | -£3,025 |
| Less: Corporation tax saved on fuel<br>5,000 miles x 15p x 4 years x 27.5% | -£825 |
| Less: Corporation tax saved on running costs<br>£2,000 - £167 x 4 years x 27.5% | -£2,016 |
| Less: VAT saved on running costs<br>£1,000 x 4 years x 20/120 | -£667 |
| **Relevant cash flows** | **-£3,083** |
| | |
| **Own Car** | |
| Income tax on net dividend in Year 1<br>£14,000 x 25% | +£3,500 |
| Less: Income tax saved on net dividend in Year 4<br>£3,000 x 25% | -£750 |
| Less: Corporation tax saved on 5,000 miles<br>5,000 x 45p x 4 years x 27.5% | -£2,475 |
| **Relevant cash flows** | **+£275** |
| | |
| **Additional cost of company car** | **-£3,358** |

Now we have a *really* significant result in favour of a company car. We can compare this example with Case Study # 2.2, where the data was identical except that annual business mileage was 15,000 instead of 5,000. The additional 10,000 business miles each year reduced the tax efficiency of a company car by exactly £2,200 over the 4 year time frame.

### Case Study 2.6 – Leasing

Our last example in the Mary Poppins green car series will look at leasing.

With leased cars there is no purchase cost, no sale proceeds and no capital allowances. Instead you just have the monthly lease rentals.

A VAT registered company will have an advantage here as it will be able to recover 50% of the VAT on the lease rentals.

Let's assume that Mary leases a 1400cc petrol-fuelled car on 6th April 2011 with a list price of £15,000 and $CO_2$ emissions of 109 g/km.

She pays for all fuel herself and drives 20,000 miles a year with fuel costs of 10p per mile. She claims 15,000 business miles a year at the maximum tax-free rates, incurs other running costs of £2,000 a year (of which £1,000 includes VAT) and expects to sell the car exactly 4 years later for £3,000.

The lease rentals over a four year term are £229.17 per month (including VAT). This is equivalent to the net capital cost of £11,000 used in Case Study # 2.1.

If Mary leases the car herself, she will need an additional dividend of £2,750 a year. We will assume that Mary pays income tax at 40% and Poppins Ltd pays corporation tax at 20%.

Should she lease the car herself or in the name of the company?

| Company Car | |
|---|---:|
| Income tax on benefit in kind<br>£15,000 x 10%/12% x 4 years x 40% tax | +£2,760 |
| Employer national insurance on benefit in kind<br>£15,000 x 10%/12% x 4 years x 13.8% | +£952 |
| Less: Corporation tax saved on employer NI<br>£952 x 20% | -£190 |
| Less: Corporation tax saved on lease rentals<br>£229.17 - £19.10 x 48 months x 20% | -£2,017 |
| Less: Corporation tax saved on fuel<br>15,000 miles x 15p x 4 years x 20% | -£1,800 |
| Less: Corporation tax saved on running costs<br>£2,000 - £167 x 4 years x 20% | -£1,466 |
| Less: VAT saved on lease rentals<br>£229.17 x 20/120 x 50% x 48 months | -£917 |
| Less: VAT saved on running costs<br>£1,000 x 4 years x 20/120 | -£667 |
| **Relevant cash flows** | **-£3,345** |
| | |
| **Own Car** | |
| Income tax on net dividends in Years 1-4<br>£2,750 x 25% x 4 years | +£2,750 |
| Less: Corporation tax saved on first 10,000 miles<br>10,000 x 45p x 4 years x 20% | -£3,600 |
| Less: Corporation tax saved on next 5,000 miles<br>5,000 x 25p x 4 years x 20% | -£1,000 |
| **Relevant cash flows** | **-£1,850** |
| | |
| **Additional cost of company car** | **-£1,495** |

We can see that the result in favour of a company car increases substantially from £761 in Case Study # 2.1 to £1,495. The extra £734 represents the VAT saved on the lease rentals of £917 less 20% corporation tax.

Of course, this example is somewhat simplistic in that we assumed the lease rentals would be equivalent to the net capital cost if Mary bought the car. That is the only way we can directly compare the 2 examples. However, it is enough to indicate that the VAT saving makes a big difference. It could well sway the decision in favour of a company car in borderline cases.

In reality the lease rentals would include a finance element as you are spreading the cost of a new car over four years. However, this can be directly compared with the cost of capital if Mary or her company bought the car outright, so it is not a particularly relevant factor unless the interest rate implicit within the lease is much higher or lower.

**Case Studies 3.1 to 3.5 – Optimal Choices**

For cars with low $CO_2$ emissions the last six case studies clearly illustrate that:

- The decision is heavily influenced by marginal tax rates (both the individual's tax rate and the company's).

- The amount of business mileage is important.

For a car with low $CO_2$ emissions, the decision is usually going to be a marginal one. Even a slight change in business use could be a material factor.

Nonetheless, it is obvious that there is generally a significant advantage to having a company car at the greener end of the spectrum.

It follows from this that there must be a point at which the balance shifts decisively towards running a company car as opposed to keeping a car in your own name. A few more examples should identify where this point lies.

### *Case Study 3.1 – Low Business Mileage*

Peter Perfect buys a Turbo Terrific on 6th April 2011 for £20,000. It has a list price of £22,000 and is petrol-fuelled with $CO_2$ emissions of 124 g/km and a 1600cc engine. He drives 5,000 business miles a year, pays for all fuel costs himself and claims mileage at the maximum tax free amounts. Running costs are £2,000 per annum (of which £1,000 includes VAT).

He will sell the car after 4 years for £5,000. He can either buy the car in the name of his company, Fall-to-Bits Ltd, or take a dividend of £20,000 to pay for it himself. If he takes the dividend he will reduce his dividend in Year 4 by £5,000 in lieu of the sale proceeds. Peter is a higher-rate taxpayer and his company pays tax at 20%. What is his most tax efficient option?

| Company Car | |
|---|---:|
| Income tax on benefit in kind<br>£22,000 x 15% x 4 years x 40% tax | +£5,280 |
| Employer national insurance on benefit in kind<br>£22,000 x 15% x 4 years x 13.8% | +£1,822 |
| Less: Corporation tax saved on employer NI<br>£1,822 x 20% | -£364 |
| Less: Capital allowances<br>£20,000 - £5,000 x 20% corporation tax | -£3,000 |
| Less: Corporation tax saved on fuel<br>5,000 miles x 18p x 4 years x 20% | -£720 |
| Less: Corporation tax saved on running costs<br>£2,000 - £167 x 4 years x 20% | -£1,466 |
| Less: VAT saved on running costs<br>£1,000 x 4 years x 20/120 | -£667 |
| **Relevant cash flows** | **+£885** |
| | |
| Own Car | |
| Income tax on net dividend in Year 1<br>£20,000 x 25% | +£5,000 |
| Less: Income tax saved on net dividend in Year 4<br>£5,000 x 25% | -£1,250 |
| Less: Corporation tax saved on 5,000 miles<br>5,000 x 45p x 4 years x 20% | -£1,800 |
| **Relevant cash flows** | **+£1,950** |
| | |
| **Additional cost of company car** | **-£1,065** |

Peter is ultimately better off with a company car by £1,065 but bear in mind that it will take several years for the capital allowances to come through because his car exceeds 110 g/km.

By Year 4 he will only have received £2,056 of the capital allowances (they go down to 18% in April 2012), which means the cash-flows are only £121 in favour of a company car at that point.

Even by Year 8 the cash-flows would only be in favour of a company car by £638. This is not large enough to make much difference and you would have to wait a very long time to reach this point.

If you allow for the time value of money by discounting future cash-flows, the result would probably be against a company car, depending on which discount rate you chose.

Judging by this example, it would appear to be quite hard to make out a financial case for buying a company car, even at relatively low $CO_2$ levels, unless you can claim the 100% enhanced capital allowance.

### *Case Study 3.2 – Classic Car*

Penelope Pitstop buys a Compact Pussycat on 6th April 2011 for £20,000 with $CO_2$ emissions of 124 g/km and a 2000cc engine.

As a classic car it is taxed on its market value, which just happens to be the same as the purchase price.

The extendable lipstick and other personal grooming accessories are tax free as the car is so old (1968 vintage for those old enough to remember the cartoons).

Penelope drives 5,000 business miles a year, pays all fuel costs herself and claims mileage at the maximum tax free amounts. Running costs are £2,000 per annum (of which £1,000 includes VAT).

She will sell the car after 4 years for £5,000. She can either buy the car in the name of her company, Girly Drivers Ltd, or take a dividend of £15,000 to pay for it herself.

If she takes the dividend she will reduce her dividend in Year 4 by £5,000 in lieu of the sale proceeds. Penelope is a higher-rate taxpayer and her company pays tax at 20%.

What is her most tax efficient option?

| Company Car | |
|---|---|
| Income tax on benefit in kind<br>£20,000 x 15% x 4 years x 40% tax | +£4,800 |
| Employer national insurance on benefit in kind<br>£20,000 x 15% x 4 years x 13.8% | +£1,656 |
| Less: Corporation tax saved on employer NI<br>£1,656 x 20% | -£331 |
| Less: Capital allowances<br>£20,000 - £5,000 x 20% corporation tax | -£3,000 |
| Less: Corporation tax saved on fuel<br>5,000 miles x 18p x 4 years x 20% | -£720 |
| Less: Corporation tax saved on running costs<br>£2,000 - £167 x 4 years x 20% | -£1,466 |
| Less: VAT saved on running costs<br>£1,000 x 4 years x 20/120 | -£667 |
| **Relevant cash flows** | **+£272** |
| | |
| **Own Car** | |
| Income tax on net dividend in Year 1<br>£20,000 x 25% | +£5,000 |
| Less: Income tax saved on net dividend in Year 4<br>£5,000 x 25% | -£1,250 |
| Less: Corporation tax saved on 5,000 miles<br>5,000 x 45p x 4 years x 20% | -£1,800 |
| **Relevant cash flows** | **+£1,950** |
| | |
| **Additional cost of company car** | **-£1,678** |

You will note that the relevant factors are identical to the previous example except that the taxable value is £2,000 lower due to it being based on market value as a classic car rather than list price. Consequently, it is much more viable for Penelope to make her Compact Pussycat a company car, because even though she waits just as long as Peter for her capital allowances to come through, the cash flows are more in her favour. We are not talking about a huge amount though. After 4 years the equation is only £734 in favour of a company car, so again you would have to discount the cash flows for future years to obtain a meaningful result.

Classic cars tend to be the exception rather than the rule, so the main purpose of this example is to demonstrate how much tax you can save by not having to use the original list price as the taxable value.

## Case Study 3.3 – Wacky Assumptions

Dick Dastardly buys a Mean Machine for £15,000 on 6th April 2011 with $CO_2$ emissions of 99 g/km and a 3000cc engine. As it is powered by a type of rocket fuel that qualifies as road fuel gas, Dick was able to get a discount off the list price so the taxable value is only £12,000. He also managed to fiddle the $CO_2$ emissions to get an abnormally low figure for a rocket fuelled car.

He drives 5,000 business miles a year, pays for all fuel costs himself and claims mileage at the maximum tax free amounts. Running costs are £5,000 per annum (£3,000 includes VAT). The car is sold after 4 years for £3,000. His company Dirty Tricks Ltd can buy the car or he can take a dividend of £15,000 to pay for it himself. He will then reduce his dividend in Year 4 by £3,000 in lieu of the sale proceeds. Dick pays tax at 40% and his company pays tax at a marginal rate of 27.5%. What is his most tax efficient option?

| Company Car | |
|---|---:|
| Income tax on benefit in kind<br>£12,000 x 10% x 4 years x 40% tax | +£1,920 |
| Employer national insurance on benefit in kind<br>£12,000 x 10% x 4 years x 13.8% | +£662 |
| Less: Corporation tax saved on employer NI<br>£662 x 27.5% | -£182 |
| Less: Capital allowances<br>£15,000 - £3,000 x 27.5% corporation tax | -£3,300 |
| Less: Corporation tax saved on fuel<br>5,000 miles x 18p x 4 years x 27.5% | -£990 |
| Less: Corporation tax saved on running costs<br>£5,000 - £500 x 4 years x 27.5% | -£4,950 |
| Less: VAT saved on running costs<br>£3,000 x 4 years x 20/120 | -£2,000 |
| **Relevant cash flows** | **-£8,840** |
| | |
| **Own Car** | |
| Income tax on net dividend in Year 1 – £15,000 x 25% | +£3,750 |
| Less: Income tax saved on net dividend in Year 4<br>£3,000 x 25% | -£750 |
| Less: Corporation tax saved on 5,000 miles<br>5,000 x 45p x 4 years x 27.5% | -£2,475 |
| **Relevant cash flows** | **+£525** |
| | |
| **Additional cost of company car** | **-£9,365** |

In this example the cash flows are hugely in favour of a company car by £9,365. However, we only achieved this amazing result by the somewhat expedient process of making sure every single relevant factor pointed in that direction. Just look at some of the crass assumptions in the above example.

First we found a way of making the taxable value lower than the purchase price. Usually the only way you can do that is by paying way more than the list price of the car, which no sane person would ever do. We also made the $CO_2$ emissions absurdly low for a 3000cc car in order to claim a 100% capital allowance in the first year and also keep the taxable benefit down to the absolute minimum for the next 4 years.

Then we kept business mileage fairly low (as in the 3 previous examples) and increased the fuel rate by having a large engine. This minimised the benefit of the 45p approved mileage rate for personally owned cars compared to the 18p advisory fuel rate for company cars running on LPG.

We increased running costs from £2,000 to an eye-watering £5,000 a year, which saves an extra £3,300 on a company car at the marginal tax rate of 27.5%. Most sensible people would get rid of a car that costs more to maintain than it is actually worth.

Finally, we assumed that Dirty Tricks Ltd pays a marginal tax rate of 27.5%, which as we have already seen makes quite a big difference. Whilst this is not an unacceptable assumption, it does tend to be fairly unusual for small owner-managed companies at present (although perhaps not in a few years time if they freeze that £300,000 threshold for much longer – the last time it went up was in 1994).

The purpose of this example is to show that it is only possible to get such a strong result in favour of a company car by stretching your imagination to its absolute limits. I used Dick Dastardly as a metaphor to cheat on the assumptions!

Certainly there are realistic circumstances where a company car is clearly the best option, but not by as much as this. In reality, it is unlikely that *all* the relevant factors would point as strongly as this towards a company car. Normally the decision would be a lot more marginal even when most of the factors are favourable.

### Case Study 3.4 – Lower CO$_2$ Levels

We're now going to look at a far more sensible example with a view to establishing exactly where it definitely becomes better to have a company car.

The next example is based on the same facts as Case Study # 3.1 except that the taxable value falls into the next CO$_2$ emission band down (115-119 g/km).

This means the car will be taxed at a different rate from April 2012 onwards as the 10% rate will apply only to cars with CO$_2$ emissions of 99 g/km or less.

Rufus Ruffcut and his beaver Sawtooth buy a Buzz Wagon for £20,000 on 6$^{th}$ April 2011 with CO$_2$ emissions of 119 g/km.

It is a petrol-fuelled car with a 1600cc engine and a list price of £22,000. Rufus drives 5,000 business miles a year, pays for all private fuel himself and claims mileage at the maximum tax-free amounts.

Running costs are £2,000 per annum (£1,000 includes VAT).

He will sell the car after 4 years for £5,000.

He can either buy the car in the name of his company, Crazy Lumberjacks Ltd, or take a dividend of £20,000 to pay for it himself.

If he takes the dividend he will reduce his dividend in Year 4 by £5,000 in lieu of the sale proceeds.

He is a higher-rate taxpayer and his company pays tax at 20%.

What is his most tax efficient option?

| Company Car | |
|---|---|
| Income tax on benefit in kind<br>£22,000 x 10%/14% x 4 years x 40% tax | +£4,576 |
| Employer national insurance on benefit in kind<br>£22,000 x 10%/14% x 4 years x 13.8% | +£1,579 |
| Less: Corporation tax saved on employer NI<br>£1,579 x 20% | -£316 |
| Less: Capital allowances<br>£20,000 - £5,000 x 20% corporation tax | -£3,000 |
| Less: Corporation tax saved on fuel<br>5,000 miles x 18p x 4 years x 20% | -£720 |
| Less: Corporation tax saved on running costs<br>£2,000 - £167 x 4 years x 20% | -£1,466 |
| Less: VAT saved on running costs<br>£1,000 x 4 years x 20/120 | -£667 |
| **Relevant cash flows** | **-£14** |
| | |
| **Own Car** | |
| Income tax on net dividend in Year 1<br>£20,000 x 25% | +£5,000 |
| Less: Corporation tax saved on net dividend in Year 4<br>£5,000 x 25% | -£1,250 |
| Less: Corporation tax saved on 5,000 miles<br>5,000 x 45p x 4 years x 20% | -£1,800 |
| **Relevant cash flows** | **+£1,950** |
| | |
| **Additional cost of company car** | **-£1,964** |

It is clearly viable for Rufus to make his Buzz Wagon a company car, even though the capital allowances will not be fully earned for many years. When the car is sold after 4 years, the relevant cash flows will be £1,020 in favour of a company car with another £657 to come from capital allowances over the next 10 years, although this does ignore the time value of money.

It looks like we are very close to the point at which a company car is almost certainly the better option, but we need to tweak a few of the other assumptions to see if that conclusion still holds good in other scenarios, specifically business mileage, maintenance costs and advisory fuel rate.

## Case Study 3.5 – Large Engine

The Ant Hill Mob buy a Bullet Proof Bomb for £20,000 on 6th April 2011 with $CO_2$ emissions of 119 g/km. It's a petrol car with a 2200cc engine. The list price is £22,000 with no optional extras (the Getaway Power facility is tax free as it is not fixed to the car). They drive 7,000 business miles a year and pay for all private fuel themselves. Running costs are £3,000 pa (£1,500 includes VAT).

They will sell the car after 4 years for £5,000. They can buy the car in the name of their company, Miniature Gangsters Ltd, or take dividends of £20,000 to pay for it themselves. In this case they can reduce their dividends in Year 4 by £5,000. They are all higher-rate taxpayers (having learnt what happened to Al Capone) and their company pays tax at 20%. What is their most tax efficient option?

| Company Car | |
|---|---:|
| Income tax on benefit in kind<br>£22,000 x 10%/14% x 4 years x 40% tax | +£4,576 |
| Employer national insurance on benefit in kind<br>£22,000 x 10%/14% x 4 years x 13.8% | +£1,579 |
| Less: Corporation tax saved on employer NI<br>£1,579 x 20% | -£316 |
| Less: Capital allowances<br>£20,000 - £5,000 x 20% corporation tax | -£3,000 |
| Less: Corporation tax saved on fuel<br>7,000 miles x 26p x 4 years x 20% | -£1,456 |
| Less: Corporation tax saved on running costs<br>£3,000 - £250 x 4 years x 20% | -£2,200 |
| Less: VAT saved on running costs<br>£1,500 x 4 years x 20/120 | -£1,000 |
| **Relevant cash flows** | **-£1,817** |
| | |
| **Own Car** | |
| Income tax on net dividend in Year 1<br>£20,000 x 25% | +£5,000 |
| Less: Income tax saved on net dividend in Year 4<br>£5,000 x 25% | -£1,250 |
| Less: Corporation tax saved on 7,000 miles<br>7,000 x 45p x 4 years x 20% | -£2,520 |
| **Relevant cash flows** | **+£1,230** |
| | |
| **Additional cost of company car** | **-£3,047** |

114

The outcome is even more positive in favour of a company car, despite the fact that higher business mileage normally makes a company car less viable. The reason it hasn't in this case is because we assumed an engine size of more than 2 litres. This allows us to use the maximum advisory fuel rate of 26p per mile rather than 18p. As the advisory fuel rates may go up over the next few years in line with prices at the pumps, this is a good way of building inflation into our case studies.

A slightly unrealistic fact here (at the time of writing) is that the car has a 2200cc engine (thus qualifying for the highest advisory fuel rate) but $CO_2$ emissions of just 119 g/km. However, it is not beyond the bounds of possibility that cars over 2 litres may come down to this level at some point.

There are already sports cars on the market with environmentally friendly credentials, such as the Volkswagen Passat 2.0 TDI (BlueMobile Tech) and the Audi A3 Cabriolet 2.0 TDI, both of which have $CO_2$ readings of only 119 g/km (source: www.comcar.co.uk). The former has a list price of just £23,375 – not a million miles out from our example. Admittedly, however, both these cars happen to be diesels, which would add 3% to their company car tax percentage.

It may also be a bit unrealistic to assume that a new car under warranty would incur running costs of £3,000 a year (especially if you refrained from taking it to a main dealer for servicing) unless of course you put an 18 year old behind the wheel and paid a bomb on the insurance!

## Case Study Analysis

It may help to compare this example with Case Studies # 3.1 and 3.4. Why are the Ant Hill Mob so much better off with a company car than either Peter Perfect or Rufus Ruffcut? Let's compare their results.

| Case Study | # 3.1 | # 3.4 | # 3.5 |
|---|---|---|---|
| Drivers | Peter Perfect | Rufus Ruffcut | Ant Hill Mob |
| List price | £22,000 | £22,000 | £22,000 |
| Purchase price | £20,000 | £20,000 | £20,000 |
| Sale proceeds | £5,000 | £5,000 | £5,000 |
| $CO_2$ (g/km) | 124 | 119 | 119 |
| Taxable percentage | 15% | 14% (10% Year 1) | 14% (10% Year 1) |
| Business mileage | 5,000 | 5,000 | 7,000 |
| Advisory fuel rate | 18p | 18p | 26p |
| Other running costs | £2,000 | £2,000 | £3,000 |
| VAT recoverable | £167 | £167 | £250 |
| Corporation tax rate | 20% | 20% | 20% |
| Income tax rate | 40% | 40% | 40% |
| | | | |
| **Company Car** | | | |
| Income tax on benefit | +£5,280 | +£4,576 | +£4,576 |
| Employer NI on benefit | +£1,822 | +£1,579 | +£1,579 |
| Less: Corporation tax saved on employer NI | -£364 | -£316 | -£316 |
| Less: Capital allowances | -£3,000 | -£3,000 | -£3,000 |
| Less: Tax saved on fuel | -£720 | -£720 | -£1,456 |
| Less: Tax saved on running costs | -£1,466 | -£1,466 | -£2,200 |
| Less: VAT saved on running costs | -£667 | -£667 | -£1,000 |
| **Relevant cash flows** | **+£885** | **-£14** | **-£1,817** |
| | | | |
| **Own Car** | | | |
| Income tax on net dividend in Year 1 | +£5,000 | +£5,000 | +£5,000 |
| Less: Income tax saved on net dividend in Year 4 | -£1,250 | -£1,250 | -£1,250 |
| Less: Corporation tax saved on mileage | -£1,800 | -£1,800 | -£2,520 |
| **Relevant cash flows** | **+£1,950** | **+£1,950** | **+£1,230** |
| | | | |
| **Additional cost of company car** | **-£1,065** | **-£1,964** | **-£3,047** |

In the first 2 cases we can see that the difference between Peter and Rufus is entirely due to a lower taxable benefit in kind.

Rufus is able to take advantage of the special 10% rate for one year before it is restricted to cars with $CO_2$ emissions of 99 g/km or less in April 2012. In fact, drivers of cars in the 115-120 g/km bracket are disproportionately affected by this change, as their tax bills will suddenly go up by 40% (or even 50% in the case of 120 g/km cars). That is quite a big hike for anyone with a company car in this category and something to think about if you are in line for a new one any time soon.

Why exactly does the Ant Hill Mob achieve an even better result for a company car than Rufus Ruffcut? We can already see that the relevant cash flows are £1,083 higher in their case and that they are caused by different figures for business mileage, running costs and advisory fuel rate, but how much does each of these factors influence the overall result?

| | |
|---|---|
| Running costs | +£1,067 |
| Business mileage | -£720 |
| Advisory fuel rate | +£736 |
| Total difference | +£1,083 |

We can see that virtually all the difference is caused by the additional running costs. An extra £1,000 a year is enough to make a company car much more viable over a 4 year time frame. But before we all rush out and buy high maintenance cars, remember the ultimate tax sin: Never pay £1 more just to save 20p tax.

### *Resale Values*

We have already looked at resale values and how these can affect the decision to go for a company car or not. Obviously they are closely aligned to the period of ownership as second-hand values tend to fall as a car gets older. Whether it is a good idea to hang on to a car for another year or so will depend on many different factors, mainly the condition and running costs of the existing vehicle, the price and availability of replacement vehicles and how quickly the car depreciates in value.

As far as the company car decision is concerned, the period of ownership can be a positive or a negative factor depending on the annual cash flows. For example, the income tax and national insurance bill on a company car is an annual cost. The tax saved on fuel/mileage and other running costs is an annual benefit. When benefits exceed costs on the Company Car side of the equation a longer period of ownership will make it more viable to choose the company car option.

High resale values tend to have a negative affect on the company car decision for two reasons. Firstly, they reduce the capital allowances that can be claimed after the car is sold.

Unlike the potentially big balancing allowance that sole traders are entitled to, a company must deduct the sales proceeds from the capital allowances 'pool' and the balance will attract writing-down allowances at 20% or 10% per year (18% or 8% from 6th April 2012) in perpetuity, so it may never receive the full allowance.

As the ability to claim capital allowances is one of the main reasons for choosing to have a company car in the first place, lower capital allowances make them less attractive compared with buying a car in your own name.

Secondly, if the car is in your name, you can keep the sale proceeds instead of having to give the money to your company. This may save you having to declare a higher dividend later, which in turn will reduce your tax bill. Low personal tax bills on dividends used to buy cars make it more attractive to keep cars in your own name.

However, never let the tax tail wag the investment dog. Cars that hold on to their value longer are obviously a good thing. Don't buy a car that depreciates quickly just because it is more tax efficient as a company vehicle!

### Case Study # 3.5 (at various resale values)

We are now going to examine how different resale values affect the calculations for the Ant Hill Mob.

Let's assume that they sell the car after 4 years, as before, but obtain sale proceeds as follows:

| Resale value after 4 years | Additional cost of company car |
|---|---|
| £4,000 | -£3,247 |
| £5,000 | -£3,047 |
| £6,000 | -£2,597 |
| £7,000 | -£2,147 |
| £8,000 | -£1,697 |

You can see from these figures that resale value can affect the outcome quite dramatically. In general, a high resale value tends to point towards keeping a car in your own name rather than making it a company car.

In this example, it is still viable to have a company car even with a very high resale value, but the decision becomes more marginal at the top end of the spectrum.

I would stress again that this analysis should not be used to decide whether to buy a car with a high resale value or not. Obviously it is always best to buy a car with a good resale value provided it is economical to buy and run.

This analysis should only be used to work out how the resale value of a car you have already bought (or decided to buy) will affect the decision on whether to make it a company car or not.

### High Company Tax Rates

We have already seen that it is much more viable to have a company car if your business pays corporation tax at a marginal rate of 27.5% rather than the usual 20% for small companies with profits under £300,000.

We will now re-examine Case Study 3.5 at a marginal tax rate of 27.5% and see how the relevant cash flows change as $CO_2$ levels increase. This will give us some idea of where the breakeven point lies.

## Case Study #3.5 at 27.5% Tax

| CO2 (g/km) | 119 | 139 | 159 | 169 | 179 | 199 |
|---|---|---|---|---|---|---|
| Taxable % from 04/2012 | 14% | 18% | 22% | 24% | 26% | 30% |
| Average % (2011-2014) | 13% | 17.75% | 21.75% | 23.75% | 25.75% | 29.75% |
| | | | | | | |
| **Company Car** | | | | | | |
| Income tax on benefit | +£4,576 | +£6,248 | +£7,656 | +£8,360 | +£9,064 | +£10,472 |
| Employer NI on benefit | +£1,579 | +£2,156 | +£2,641 | +£2,884 | +£3,127 | +£3,613 |
| Less: Tax saved on employer NI | -£434 | -£593 | -£726 | -£793 | -£860 | -£994 |
| Less: Capital allowances | -£4,125 | -£4,125 | -£4,125 | -£4,125 | -£4,125 | -£4,125 |
| Less: Tax saved on fuel | -£2,002 | -£2,002 | -£2,002 | -£2,002 | -£2,002 | -£2,002 |
| Less: Tax saved on running costs | -£3,025 | -£3,025 | -£3,025 | -£3,025 | -£3,025 | -£3,025 |
| Less: VAT saved on running costs | -£1,000 | -£1,000 | -£1,000 | -£1,000 | -£1,000 | -£1,000 |
| **Relevant cash flows** | **-£4,431** | **-£2,341** | **-£581** | **+£299** | **+£1,179** | **+£2,939** |
| | | | | | | |
| **Own Car** | | | | | | |
| Income tax on net dividend in Year 1 | +£5,000 | +£5,000 | +£5,000 | +£5,000 | +£5,000 | +£5,000 |
| Less: Tax saved on net dividend in Year 4 | -£1,250 | -£1,250 | -£1,250 | -£1,250 | -£1,250 | -£1,250 |
| Less: Tax saved on mileage | -£3,465 | -£3,465 | -£3,465 | -£3,465 | -£3,465 | -£3,465 |
| **Relevant cash flows** | **+£285** | **+£285** | **+£285** | **+£285** | **+£285** | **+£285** |
| | | | | | | |
| **Extra cost of company car** | **-£4,716** | **-£2,626** | **-£866** | **+£14** | **+£894** | **+£2,654** |

Remember here that the car was actually purchased on 6th April 2011, so at 119 g/km it benefits from the old 10% band in Year 1 as this covered petrol-fuelled cars up to 120 g/km (diesels are 3% higher). At the higher $CO_2$ levels, the Taxable Percentage is 1% lower in Year 1 than shown above.

We must also remember that the marginal tax rate for the company will be 27.5% only in 2011/12.

For the next 3 years it will gradually go down, so the relevant cash flows will be slightly different to those shown above. However, this does not materially affect the outcome.

**We can see from this that it only stops being beneficial to choose the company car option when $CO_2$ levels are at the 169 g/km mark. Taking the time value of money into account, the real breakeven point would be around the 160 g/km mark.**

**This is much higher than for small companies paying 20% tax where the breakeven point is typically at the 120-124 g/km band.**

However, that is just a general rule of thumb, and you should always consider the influence of other factors such as business mileage, running costs, list price, re-sale values and your own personal tax rate.

## Ten Lessons

To conclude this chapter, let's recap the lessons we've learned if you want a company car to work out cheaper for you:

### *Lesson # 1 – Going Green*

A company car is far more likely to be beneficial if you go green. The lower your $CO_2$ emissions the lower your tax bill on the benefit-in-kind is likely to be.

### *Lesson # 2 – Higher-rate Tax*

A company car is more likely to work out cheaper for you as an *owner-manager* if you are a higher-rate taxpayer. It is not entirely impossible for you to be better off with a company car if you are a basic-rate taxpayer (Case Study # 2.4 proves that you can), but if you do not have to pay tax on your dividends, it is probably better for you to take the money you need to pay for a car out of your company as a dividend and buy it in your own name.

### *Lesson # 3 – Corporation Tax*

You are far more likely to be better off with a company car if your business pays high marginal rates of corporation tax, which usually means making taxable profits of at least £300,000 per annum.

### *Lesson # 4 – Business Mileage*

You may be better off *not* having a company car if you do a lot of business mileage. At present the advisory fuel rates for company car users are still much lower than the approved mileage rates for those who use their own cars. So if you happen to do a lot of business miles in the course of your work, you may be better off putting the car in your own name.

### Lesson # 5 – Insurance and Maintenance

High insurance premiums and garage bills may be unavoidable, but at least with a company car you can claim them against corporation tax, which you cannot do if the car is in your name. The approved mileage rates for employees are deemed to cover *all* running costs, so you cannot claim anything else against tax.

### Lesson # 6 – Capital Allowances

If your car has $CO_2$ emissions of 110 g/km or less you will qualify for a 100% enhanced capital allowance in the year of purchase. It may therefore be beneficial to buy such a car in the name of the company although there will be a balancing charge to pay when you sell it.

Cars above 160 g/km only get capital allowances at 10% per annum (going down to 8% in April 2012) so they are unlikely to be attractive to business owners as company cars although that would probably be the case anyway given the relatively high tax rates on them.

### Lesson # 7 – Resale Value

Sometimes it is better to keep a car with a high resale value in your own name rather than make it a company car, as capital allowances will be lower. You can then reduce dividends from your company when you sell the car and thus pay less income tax, as you can keep the sale proceeds.

### Lesson # 8 – Period of Ownership

A short period of ownership *may* make it more advantageous to have a company car as the number of years you have to pay tax on the benefit is reduced, but obviously that will only be true if you do not replace it with another company car. At the same time, the resale value will be higher and capital allowances would consequently be lower, which tends to point away from company cars. Period of ownership is usually therefore inconclusive.

### Lesson # 9 – The Price Cap

The £80,000 cap on the list price of company cars was scrapped with effect from April 2011, so this no longer acts as an incentive to buy super-luxury cars in the company name. However, if you can afford to buy such a car in the first place, you are not likely to worry about the tax consequences!

### Lesson # 10 – VAT

A VAT registered business can recover 100% of the VAT on all maintenance bills and 50% of the VAT on lease rentals. A director using his own car and claiming mileage from his company cannot recover any VAT at all. Therefore, a company car may be more tax efficient if your company is VAT registered, although not if you are on the flat rate scheme.

# Chapter 9

# Decision # 2 - Should I Claim for Mileage or Running Costs?

If you are a sole trader or work through a partnership, you don't have to worry about the company car rules in respect of your own vehicle. Your employees may well have to pay tax on a car benefit if you provide them with a vehicle, but you do not.

However, you may have to choose between claiming tax relief on your business mileage and claiming tax relief on a proportion of your running costs, including capital allowances.

Actually this choice is only available to self-employed people with annual turnover up to £73,000. If your turnover is above this limit you cannot claim mileage rates – you have to claim tax relief on your actual motoring expenses. £73,000 is the same as the current VAT registration threshold and goes up every year, but this is just a convenient limit and has nothing to do with VAT itself.

If you start using mileage rates and your turnover subsequently exceeds the threshold, you may continue using mileage rates until that particular vehicle is no longer used in your business. For any new vehicles used in your business, however, you would have to claim capital allowances and a proportion of running costs instead. As we shall see, this is probably to your advantage.

So what is best – the mileage rates or the running costs? It depends on a number of factors:

- Total running costs
- The mileage rates
- Your business mileage
- Your business use proportion
- The purchase cost of your car (or lease rentals)
- Your car's $CO_2$ emissions

We will now look at all these factors in the paragraphs below.

# Running Costs and Mileage

Total running costs include fuel, maintenance, insurance, road tax and any other costs that relate to the car itself as opposed to your use of it, such as parking. The higher your running costs, the more likely it will be that you are better off claiming actual running costs rather than mileage.

As we know, the mileage rates are fixed at 45p per mile for the first 10,000 miles in the 2011/12 tax year and 25p per mile above that.

You can also claim an extra 5p per mile for passengers.

The mileage rates are meant to cover ALL motoring costs, including depreciation, so you cannot claim anything else apart from parking, road tolls and a share of the finance costs (if any).

Your business use proportion is also important as it determines the share of the running costs you can claim.

For example, if you drive 12,000 miles a year and 6,000 are for business (excluding ordinary commuting) then you can claim 50% of your running costs and capital allowances.

Generally speaking, the higher the business use percentage, the better it is to claiming actual running costs.

# Capital Allowances

If you choose to claim mileage rates then no capital allowance claim is allowed on the purchase price of the car. It follows from this that it is more worthwhile claiming capital allowances on expensive cars than cheaper ones.

The car's $CO_2$ emissions will determine the size of your capital allowance claim. Cars with $CO_2$ emissions up to 110 g/km qualify for 100% enhanced capital allowances in the year of purchase.

Self-employed business owners (sole traders and partners) do not have to pay benefit-in-kind charges on their cars BUT they must reduce their capital allowance claims to reflect private use of their cars, normally on a mileage basis.

For example, if the car is used 50% for business and 50% privately, half the cost of the car can be claimed as an income tax deduction.

Cars with $CO_2$ emissions between 111-160 g/km only qualify for 20% writing-down allowances each year (which will reduce to 18% from 6th April 2012). Cars above 160 g/km only qualify for 10% allowances (reducing to 8% from 6th April 2012).

Sole traders and partners have an advantage over their limited company counterparts when it comes to cars as sole traders and partners can claim balancing allowances when they eventually sell them (providing the car has **some** private use by the proprietor or partners and is not available for the private use of employees).

A balancing allowance is in effect a large 'catch-up' tax deduction.

### Example

For example, suppose a sole trader buys a car with $CO_2$ emissions of 140 g/km on 6th April 2011 for £20,000 and sells it on 6th April 2016 for £5,000.

The car qualifies for 20% writing-down allowances. His business use proportion is 60%. His net capital cost over the period of ownership will be £15,000 of which 60% (£9,000) is tax deductible. Over the five years he will claim capital allowances of £7,660 so he will be entitled to a balancing allowance on disposal of £1,340.

However, suppose the car has $CO_2$ emissions of 110 g/km. He would then claim an enhanced capital allowance of £12,000 in the year of purchase (£20,000 reduced by 40% private use), so he would have a balancing charge of £3,000 in the year of disposal.

As noted above, balancing allowances are generally only available to sole traders or partners for cars that have some private use. If the car was used 100% for business then it would have to go into the main pool for plant and machinery as there are no private use reductions. This means that no balancing allowance would be available – you would simply deduct the sale proceeds from the pool balance and continue claiming writing-down allowances each year *ad infinitum*.

Therefore, it is always worthwhile making sure a car has at least 1% private use, perhaps by taking it to the shops once a year, so you can keep it out of the main pool.

## Leased Cars

For leased cars you must disallow 15% of the rental charges against tax for cars with $CO_2$ emissions above 160 g/km, but only if they have been leased since April 2009.

For example, suppose you lease a car with $CO_2$ emissions of 175 g/km for £200 a month. Only £170 per month could be claimed against tax.

This is fairly easy to understand but the formula you have to follow for cars leased prior to 1st April 2009 is a bit more complicated, or at least it is for cars with a list price exceeding £12,000.

Up to £12,000 you can claim 100% of your lease rentals against tax. If the list price exceeds £12,000 then you must disallow 50% of the lease rentals against tax for the balance above £12,000 on a pro-rata basis.

For example, suppose you leased a car with a list price of £15,000 at £200 per month. The balance above £12,000 is obviously £3,000. This is 20% of the list price so 20% of the lease rentals are subject to the 50% abatement. Therefore, you must disallow £20 per month:

$$£200 \times 20\% \times 50\% = £20 \text{ per month}$$

## Case Studies 4.1 to 4.5

Putting all this information together, we can work out whether self-employed business owners should claim mileage or running costs. The following case studies will illustrate how the various factors affect the decision.

### *Case Study # 4.1*

Jack, a sole trader, buys a car on 6th April 2011 for £20,000 with $CO_2$ emissions of 140 g/km and running costs (including fuel) of £4,000 per annum.

He drives a total of 12,000 miles a year of which 6,000 are for business.

He sells it after 5 years for £5,000. Should he claim the mileage rates or running costs?

| Mileage | |
|---|---|
| 6,000 miles x 45p x 5 years | £13,500 |
| | |
| **Running costs** | |
| Capital allowance – 2011/12 (£20,000 x 20% x 50%) | £2,000 |
| Capital allowance – 2012/13 (£16,000 x 18% x 50%) | £1,440 |
| Capital allowance – 2013/14 (£13,120 x 18% x 50%) | £1,181 |
| Capital allowance – 2014/15 (£10,758 x 18% x 50%) | £968 |
| Capital allowance – 2015/16 (£8,822 x 18% x 50%) | £794 |
| Balancing allowance (£15,000 x 50% - £6,383) | £1,117 |
| Running costs (£4,000 x 50% x 5 years) | £10,000 |
| Total claimed against tax | £17,500 |
| | |
| **Additional benefit of claiming running costs** | **£4,000** |

We can see here that Jack is better off claiming capital allowances and a share of the running costs rather than the mileage rates.

If he is a higher-rate taxpayer he would save £1,600 in income tax (£4,000 x 40%) over the 5 years.

## Case Study # 4.2

Jim, a sole trader, buys a car on 6$^{th}$ April 2011 for £20,000 with $CO_2$ emissions of 140 g/km and running costs (including fuel) of £5,500 per annum.

He drives a total of 20,000 miles a year of which 5,000 are for business.

He sells it after 5 years for £5,000.

Should he claim for mileage or running costs?

| Mileage | |
|---|---|
| 5,000 miles x 45p x 5 years | £11,250 |
| | |
| **Running costs** | |
| Capital allowance – 2011/12 (£20,000 x 20% x 25%) | £1,000 |
| Capital allowance – 2012/13 (£16,000 x 18% x 25%) | £720 |
| Capital allowance – 2013/14 (£13,120 x 18% x 25%) | £590 |
| Capital allowance – 2014/15 (£10,758 x 18% x 25%) | £484 |
| Capital allowance – 2015/16 (£8,822 x 18% x 25%) | £397 |
| Balancing allowance (£15,000 x 25% - £3,191) | £559 |
| Running costs (£5,500 x 25% x 5 years) | £6,875 |
| Total claimed against tax | £10,625 |
| | |
| **Additional benefit of claiming mileage** | **£625** |

Here we have the opposite result. Jim is better off claiming mileage, but only marginally.

He should therefore take account of the fact that running costs could increase significantly over 5 years, especially fuel, whereas the main 45p mileage rate could be frozen for many years.

Will it be raised again any time soon? Maybe, but it seems unlikely that the approved mileage rates will keep pace with fuel price inflation in the long term.

## Case Study # 4.3

John, a sole trader, buys a car on $6^{th}$ April 2011 for £12,000 with $CO_2$ emissions of 110 g/km and running costs (including fuel) of £3,500 per annum.

He drives a total of 12,000 miles a year of which 8,000 are for business.

He sells it after 5 years for £2,000.

Should he claim for mileage or running costs?

| Mileage | |
|---|---|
| 8,000 miles x 45p x 5 years | +£18,000 |
| | |
| **Running costs** | |
| Capital allowance 2011/12 (£12,000 x 100% x 80%) | +£9,600 |
| Less: Balancing charge (£10,000 x 80% - £9,600) | -£1,600 |
| Running costs (£3,500 x 80% x 5 years) | +£14,000 |
| Total claimed against tax | +£22,000 |
| | |
| **Additional benefit of claiming running costs** | **+£4,000** |

In this example, a cheap car is combined with high business use.

The capital allowance is therefore unaffected to a large degree and the result clearly shows that John should claim running costs rather than mileage.

### Case Study # 4.4

Jed, a sole trader, buys a second hand car on 6<sup>th</sup> April 2011 for £10,000 with $CO_2$ emissions of 170 g/km and running costs (including fuel) of £7,000 per annum.

He drives a total of 30,000 miles a year of which 9,000 are for business.

He sells it after 5 years for £1,000.

Should he claim for mileage or running costs?

| Mileage | |
|---|---|
| 9,000 miles x 45p x 5 years | £20,250 |
|  |  |
| **Running costs** | |
| Capital allowance – 2011/12 (£10,000 x 10% x 30%) | £300 |
| Capital allowance – 2012/13 (£9,000 x 8% x 30%) | £216 |
| Capital allowance – 2013/14 (£8,280 x 8% x 30%) | £199 |
| Capital allowance – 2014/15 (£7,618 x 8% x 30%) | £183 |
| Capital allowance – 2015/16 (£7,008 x 8% x 30%) | £168 |
| Balancing allowance (£9,000 x 30% - £1,066) | £1,634 |
| Running costs (£7,000 x 30% x 5 years) | £10,500 |
| Total claimed against tax | £13,200 |
|  |  |
| **Additional benefit of claiming mileage** | **£7,050** |

Here the result is hugely in favour of claiming mileage.

Why is that so when two of the other examples indicate clearly that it is better to claim running costs?

Well this example is slightly unusual in that the car has a low purchase price and high business mileage but a relatively low business use proportion.

132

## Case Study # 4.5

Jan, a sole trader, leases a car for three years on 6<sup>th</sup> April 2011 and pays monthly rentals of £400 (excluding VAT).

The car has $CO_2$ emissions of 170 g/km and running costs (including fuel) of £6,000 per annum.

She drives a total of 24,000 miles a year of which 9,600 (40%) is for business.

Should she claim for mileage or running costs?

| Mileage | |
|---|---|
| 9,600 miles x 45p x 3 years | +£12,960 |
| | |
| **Running costs** | |
| Lease rentals (£400 x 36 months x 85% x 40% ) | +£4,896 |
| Running costs (£6,000 x 40% x 3 years) | +£7,200 |
| Total claimed against tax | +£12,096 |
| | |
| **Additional benefit of claiming mileage** | **+£864** |

In this example the business use proportion is higher but 15% of the lease rentals are disallowed.

The result is in favour of mileage but by nowhere near as much as in the previous example.

Against this, Jan would have to consider the affect of inflation on running costs and the risk of the mileage rates remaining frozen.

## Summary

In general it is better for sole traders and partnerships to claim their actual motoring costs (capital allowances and a share of the running costs) rather than using the mileage rates.

Remember those whose turnover exceeds £73,000 generally cannot use the mileage rates anyway.

Using the mileage rates may be better where business mileage is high but the business use proportion is fairly low.

The mileage rates may also be advantageous where capital allowances are very low (over the whole life of the vehicle).

Remember, once you have decided which method to use for a particular vehicle, you must stick with it while you still have that vehicle.

However, there is nothing to stop you using different methods for different vehicles. This may come in handy if a particular vehicle is only used occasionally for business purposes or has very low running costs.

One error you should avoid is thinking it is not worth claiming capital allowances on cars with $CO_2$ emissions above 160 g/km and that the mileage rates must therefore be more tax efficient.

It is true that capital allowances can only be claimed at 10% per annum (or 8% from April 2012) on these vehicles BUT, as a sole trader, you will get a balancing allowance when you sell the car, so you will get full tax relief on the net capital cost in the end.

# Chapter 10

# Decision # 3 - Should My Company Pay for Private Fuel?

If you run your own company, it is rarely a good idea to put *all* your fuel bills through the company. That is because the corporation tax savings on the fuel will rarely outweigh the tax and employer national insurance on the fuel benefit-in-kind. The following case study illustrates this.

## Case Study # 5.1

Del Boy works through his own company, Fools and Horses Limited, and drives a petrol-fuelled company car with $CO_2$ emissions of 150 g/km.

The taxable benefit-in-kind (BIK) for 2011/12 is therefore 20% of list price.

He drives 12,000 miles a year of which 6,000 are for business. Petrol is £1.35 a litre and his car does an average of 30 miles to the gallon (or 6.6 miles to the litre).

The fuel benefit for 2011/12 is £18,800 and he is a basic-rate taxpayer. His company pays corporation tax at 20% and the advisory fuel rate for business mileage is 18p.

Would Del-Boy be better off paying for private fuel himself?

We will assume that if he does pay for private fuel himself he will need to extract an equivalent amount from the company as extra dividend but that this will be tax free as he will still be below the higher-rate threshold. Therefore, the funding aspect does not affect the calculations.

| Company pays for private fuel | |
| :--- | ---: |
| Tax on fuel benefit<br>£18,800 x 20% BIK x 20% income tax | +£752 |
| Employer national insurance on fuel benefit<br>£18,800 x 20% BIK x 13.8% | +£519 |
| Less: Corporation tax saved on employer NI<br>£519 x 20% | -£104 |
| Cost of fuel (12,000/6.6 x £1.35) | +£2,455 |
| Less: Corporation tax saved on fuel (£2,455 x 20%) | -£491 |
| Total cost | +£3,131 |
| | |
| **Del-Boy pays for private fuel** | |
| Cost of fuel (12,000/6.6 x £1.35) | +£2,455 |
| Less: Corporation tax saved on business mileage<br>£6,000 x 18p x 20% | -£216 |
| Total cost | +£2,239 |
| | |
| **Additional cost of fuel benefit** | **+£892** |

The first three items in this equation are fixed amounts as the fuel benefit remains the same no matter how much money is actually spent on fuel. The cost of fuel also does not affect the outcome as this will be the same whichever decision Del-Boy makes.

It all boils down to how much corporation tax can be saved on:

- The fuel costs – currently £491
- The business mileage – currently £216

If we assume that business travel remains the same at 6,000 miles and the advisory fuel rate is 18p, the tax saved on mileage is fixed at £216.

This means the corporation tax saving on total fuel costs needs to go up to £1,383 (being £491 + £892). As corporation tax is 20%, this would require total fuel costs to be £6,915.

Therefore, at £1.35 per litre and 6.6 litres to a mile, total mileage would need to be 33,807 per annum of which 27,807 would be private mileage.

## Analysis

Whilst it is not impossible to drive this number of miles in a year, you would need to either live a long way from your work or have a very busy social life.

If you drove 60 miles to work and then 60 miles back home again, 5 days a week and 47 weeks a year, you would clock up 28,200 miles. And obviously the more petrol goes up in price the more tax-efficient it becomes to put all fuel costs through the company.

However, business mileage in a company car that is reimbursed to an employee can be claimed against corporation tax anyway at the advisory fuel rates, so if the car is used a lot for your work (as opposed to commuting to work) you would almost certainly be better off as an owner-director paying for all private fuel yourself.

# Chapter 11

# Decision # 4
# How Should I Claim VAT on Fuel?

## The 3 Methods

As we know only too well, petrol and diesel are very heavily taxed and a huge proportion of the price at the pumps ends up in the hands of the Chancellor (around 60%).

Most of this is fuel duty, but it also includes VAT at the standard rate of 20%. This is recoverable as input tax by all businesses that are VAT registered.

Basically, there are 3 different ways of claiming back VAT on fuel:

- **Method A**
  Claim VAT on ALL fuel purchased (including private fuel) and pay output tax using the Fuel Scale Charges

- **Method B**
  Only claim back VAT on fuel used for business purposes

- **Method C**
  Calculate VAT on business mileage using the HMRC advisory fuel rates (not the actual fuel costs)

There is a fourth option: do not claim any VAT on fuel at all! If the amount of VAT you can reclaim is negligible, you may prefer not to bother reclaiming it just to avoid having to keep fuel receipts.

However, if your private mileage is very high, you may find it advantageous to use Method A.

For businesses that are not VAT registered or employees using their own cars for work, the position is quite simple: VAT cannot be claimed back at all. The same goes for businesses operating the VAT flat rate scheme as no input tax is generally recoverable.

# Analysis of the 3 Methods

## Method A – Fuel Scale Charges

### *Companies*

This method is mandatory if the company pays for the private fuel of employees and does not require reimbursement at or above the advisory fuel rates.

This normally only happens with company cars but can also be applicable if you give employees fuel cards to use their own cars for work.

### *Sole Traders/Partnerships*

Sole traders and partners will also need to pay the fuel scale charge if they claim back VAT on **all** their fuel (private and business) without working out the business use proportion.

## Method B – Input Tax Restriction

### *Sole Traders/Partnerships*

This is the normal method of accounting for VAT by sole traders and partnerships.

Most already claim their motoring costs against tax according to the business use proportion for each vehicle (e.g. 40% or 50%), so it is fairly straightforward to use the same fraction for claiming back VAT on fuel.

Obviously if the car is used 100% for business then there will be no need to reduce the VAT claim. However, sole traders and partners should always make sure there is at least 1% private use on cars with $CO_2$ emissions above 110 g/km so that they can claim a balancing allowance when they sell the car.

### *Companies*

Companies can also use this method if they require employees to reimburse private mileage at or above the advisory fuel rates.

### Method C – Mileage Claims

#### *Companies*

This method is only applicable where you reimburse business mileage expenses of your employees.

This will generally apply to smaller businesses that do not run their own fleets and rely on employees using their own vehicles for business journeys.

It also applies to company cars where employees pay for all fuel themselves and then claim for business mileage.

Owner-managed companies need to use this method if, as is often the case, it is not worth having a company car. Whatever rate you pay for mileage, you must only claim VAT on the advisory fuel rates unless you can prove a different figure is more appropriate.

#### *Sole Traders/Partnerships*

Interestingly there is no mileage option for sole traders and partnerships with turnover below the VAT threshold as there is for income tax deductions.

You might think that the VAT treatment would mirror the income tax treatment, but VAT Notice 700/64 (Motoring Expenses) is very explicit as to the methods allowed for claiming back input tax on fuel (as set out in paragraph 8.1 of that Notice).

The approved mileage rates are not among them. These are only relevant if you actually pay your employees mileage for using their own cars.

We can see from the above that the only real choice is between Methods A and B since Method C is restricted to expense claims. Even then this choice is only available if the employer does not pay for the private fuel of employees.

If you **do** pay for the private fuel of employees then Method A is mandatory even if you know what the business element was and would rather use Method B instead.

That is because you are making a taxable supply to the employee and you must therefore account for output tax on it.

If you need to use Method C on a particular car, then you do not have the option of using Methods A or B on that car, or vice versa.

However, if your business pays for fuel on some cars and mileage on others, it is possible that you could use all 3 methods simultaneously.

Given that you need to keep VAT receipts even for cars on which you pay mileage, you obviously need to make sure you can tell which receipts are for which cars.

The best way of doing this is simply to write the registration number on each receipt. With fuel cards it is easier as the statements should show the registration number for each purchase.

# VAT Fuel Scale Rates

The VAT fuel scale rates are published periodically by HM Revenue & Customs and can be looked up on their website.

The rates at the time of writing have been in force since 1 May 2011 and are as follows.

## VAT Fuel Scale Charges

| CO2 Emissions | Monthly (£) | Quarterly (£) | Annual (£) |
|---|---|---|---|
| Up to 120g/km | 8.67 | 26.17 | 105.00 |
| 125 g/km | 13.00 | 39.33 | 157.50 |
| 130 g/km | 14.00 | 42.00 | 168.33 |
| 135 g/km | 14.83 | 44.67 | 178.33 |
| 140 g/km | 15.67 | 47.17 | 189.17 |
| 145 g/km | 16.50 | 49.83 | 200.00 |
| 150 g/km | 17.50 | 52.50 | 210.00 |
| 155 g/km | 18.33 | 55.17 | 220.83 |
| 160 g/km | 19.17 | 57.67 | 230.83 |
| 165 g/km | 20.00 | 60.33 | 241.67 |
| 170 g/km | 21.00 | 63.00 | 252.50 |
| 175 g/km | 21.83 | 65.67 | 262.50 |
| 180 g/km | 22.67 | 68.17 | 273.33 |
| 185 g/km | 23.50 | 70.83 | 284.17 |
| 190 g/km | 24.50 | 73.50 | 294.17 |
| 195 g/km | 25.33 | 76.17 | 305.00 |
| 200 g/km | 26.17 | 78.67 | 315.00 |
| 205 g/km | 27.00 | 81.33 | 325.83 |
| 210 g/km | 28.00 | 84.00 | 336.67 |
| 215 g/km | 28.83 | 86.67 | 346.67 |
| 220 g/km | 29.67 | 89.33 | 357.50 |
| 225 g/km | 30.50 | 91.83 | 367.50 |

If the $CO_2$ emissions are not a multiple of 5, always round down to the next figure. Bi-fuel cars with more than one $CO_2$ reading should always be based on the lower figure. If a car is so old that it does not have an official $CO_2$ reading, the scale charge should be based on cylinder capacity as follows:

Up to 1400cc      140 g/km
1401-2000cc       175 g/km
Above 2000cc      225 g/km

You will see that the figures relate to the $CO_2$ emissions of the vehicle and represent the amounts of output tax to be paid per vehicle for monthly, quarterly or annual VAT returns. As they are fixed rates, it does not matter how much the fuel actually cost or what the level of private mileage was.

It therefore follows that the scale rates become more tax efficient as fuel prices and/or private mileage increase. A few examples will illustrate this effect.

## Case Studies 6.1 to 6.3

The following Case Studies look at whether it is better to use Method A or Method B to recover VAT on fuel.

### Case Study 6.1

Bob is a sole trader and owns a petrol car with $CO_2$ emissions of 158 g/km. He drives a total of 12,000 miles a year of which 5,000 are for business. Petrol costs £1.35 per litre and his car does an average of 30 miles to the gallon (or 6.6 miles to the litre). He does quarterly VAT returns.

Should he reclaim all the VAT on his fuel and pay the fuel scale charge or only claim back the VAT on fuel used for business purposes?

| Scale charges (Method A) | |
|---|---|
| Input tax = 12,000 miles x £1.35/6.6 x 20/120 | +£409.09 |
| Output tax = £55.17 x 4 quarters | -£220.68 |
| Net recoverable VAT | +£188.41 |
| | |
| **Claiming VAT on Business Fuel (Method B)** | |
| 12,000 miles x £1.35/6.6 x 5/12 x 20/120 | +£170.45 |
| | |
| **Additional benefit of Method A** | **+£17.96** |

Bob is roughly £18 a year better off paying the Fuel Scale Charge. However, this VAT saving will disappear if his business mileage goes up or his private mileage goes down. It will also be affected by changes in fuel prices or the average fuel consumption of his car (say if he does more motorway driving). He needs to keep track of his fuel bills and mileage records to ensure he does not end up paying too much VAT in the long run.

### Case Study 6.2

Bill is a sole trader and owns a diesel car with $CO_2$ emissions of 143 g/km. He drives a total of 12,000 miles a year of which 6,000 are for business. Diesel costs £1.42 per litre and his car does an average of 40 miles to the gallon (or 8.8 miles to the litre). He does quarterly VAT returns.

Should he reclaim all the VAT on his fuel and pay the fuel scale charge or only claim back the VAT on fuel used for business purposes?

| Scale charges (Method A) | |
|---|---|
| Input tax = 12,000 miles x £1.42/8.8 x 20/120 | +£322.73 |
| Output tax = £47.17 x 4 quarters | -£188.68 |
| Net recoverable VAT | +£134.05 |
| | |
| **Claiming VAT on Business Fuel (Method B)** | |
| 12,000 miles x £1.42/8.8 x 6/12 x 20/120 | +£161.36 |
| | |
| **Additional benefit of Method B** | **+£27.31** |

Bill is £27 a year better off *not* paying the Fuel Scale Charge and claiming VAT on his business mileage.

Even though his business use proportion is slightly higher than Bob's and diesel costs more, the superior fuel economy of his car means that he pays less for fuel, so input tax is lower.

The fuel scale charges are the same for both petrol and diesel so in this case they work against him even though they are lower for his car. The differential is about 20% of his net recoverable VAT so is less likely to be affected by changes in fuel prices, fuel consumption or mileage in the short term. Even so he should keep track of his fuel costs and mileage.

144

## Case Study 6.3

Ben has a limited company and employs a team of five salesmen who all drive company cars (petrol fuelled) with $CO_2$ emissions of 130 g/km. Each salesman drives around 20,000 miles a year of which 12,000 are for business. The salesmen pay for all petrol using corporate fuel cards and then reimburse non-business mileage to the company at the advisory fuel rates. Petrol costs £1.35 per litre and the cars do an average of 40 miles to the gallon (or 8.8 miles to the litre). Ben does quarterly VAT returns. How much VAT can re-claim?

| Scale charges (Method A) | |
|---|---|
| Input tax = 20,000 miles x £1.35/8.8 x 5 x 20/120 | +£2,556.82 |
| Output tax = £42.00 x 4 quarters x 5 | -£840.00 |
| Net recoverable VAT | +£1,716.82 |
| | |
| **Restricted input tax (Method B)** | |
| 20,000 miles x £1.35/8.8 x 12/20 x 5 x 20/120 | +£1,534.09 |
| | |
| **Additional benefit of Method A** | **+£182.73** |

The company is better off by £183 a year (or £36 per car) paying the Fuel Scale Charge. However, the differential is only 10.6% of the net recoverable VAT so this could easily change.

Note that Ben only has a choice between Methods A and B because he requires reimbursement of private mileage. If he did not, then Method A would be mandatory as he is making a taxable supply.

## Summary and Tables

It seems that in most cases there is very little difference between paying output tax on the fuel scale rates and restricting your input tax on fuel costs. It is only when private use of a car is very low that it becomes particularly worthwhile to use Method B.

The main beneficiaries of the scale rates are large fleet operators who give their employees fuel cards without any reimbursement of private mileage. Obviously it saves them a lot of admin work.

For owners of cars with $CO_2$ emissions above say 200 g/km, paying the fuel scale charges can still be more expensive than restricting input tax, even when private mileage is about average.

Say you drive 7,000 non-business miles a year in a car with $CO_2$ emissions of 225 g/km. Output tax would be £367.32. If petrol costs £1.35 per litre and the car does only 5 miles to the litre, the input tax on that private mileage would be £315. Therefore you would be £52 per annum worse off paying the fuel scale charges.

The following tables will help you choose between Method A or B at various fuel prices and $CO_2$ emission levels.

**If your private mileage is higher than the figures in these tables you should always pay the Fuel Scale Charge. If it is less, then you should consider opting for the input tax restriction instead.**

### Minimum Private Mileage for VAT Fuel Scale Rates (Petrol)

| CO2 Emissions | Quarterly Scale chg | Average MPG | Price of unleaded petrol per litre | | | | | | | | |
|---|---|---|---|---|---|---|---|---|---|---|---|
| | | | £1.20 | £1.25 | £1.30 | £1.35 | £1.40 | £1.45 | £1.50 | £1.55 | £1.60 |
| <120g/km | £26.17 | 50 | 5,757 | 5,526 | 5,314 | 5,117 | 4,934 | 4,764 | 4,605 | 4,457 | 4,318 |
| 125 g/km | £39.33 | 45 | 7,786 | 7,475 | 7,187 | 6,921 | 6,674 | 6,444 | 6,229 | 6,028 | 5,840 |
| 130 g/km | £42.00 | 41 | 7,576 | 7,273 | 6,993 | 6,734 | 6,494 | 6,270 | 6,061 | 5,865 | 5,682 |
| 135 g/km | £44.67 | 40 | 7,861 | 7,547 | 7,256 | 6,988 | 6,738 | 6,506 | 6,289 | 6,086 | 5,896 |
| 140 g/km | £47.17 | 39 | 8,093 | 7,770 | 7,471 | 7,194 | 6,937 | 6,698 | 6,475 | 6,266 | 6,070 |
| 145 g/km | £49.83 | 38 | 8,331 | 7,997 | 7,690 | 7,405 | 7,140 | 6,894 | 6,664 | 6,449 | 6,248 |
| 150 g/km | £52.50 | 37 | 8,546 | 8,204 | 7,889 | 7,596 | 7,325 | 7,073 | 6,837 | 6,616 | 6,409 |
| 155 g/km | £55.17 | 36 | 8,738 | 8,388 | 8,066 | 7,767 | 7,490 | 7,231 | 6,990 | 6,765 | 6,553 |
| 160 g/km | £57.67 | 35 | 8,880 | 8,525 | 8,197 | 7,893 | 7,612 | 7,349 | 7,104 | 6,875 | 6,660 |
| 165 g/km | £60.33 | 34 | 9,024 | 8,663 | 8,330 | 8,022 | 7,735 | 7,468 | 7,219 | 6,987 | 6,768 |
| 170 g/km | £63.00 | 33 | 9,147 | 8,781 | 8,443 | 8,130 | 7,840 | 7,570 | 7,317 | 7,081 | 6,860 |
| 175 g/km | £65.67 | 32 | 9,245 | 8,875 | 8,534 | 8,218 | 7,924 | 7,651 | 7,396 | 7,158 | 6,934 |
| 180 g/km | £68.17 | 31 | 9,297 | 8,925 | 8,582 | 8,264 | 7,969 | 7,694 | 7,438 | 7,198 | 6,973 |
| 185 g/km | £70.83 | 30 | 9,348 | 8,975 | 8,629 | 8,310 | 8,013 | 7,737 | 7,479 | 7,238 | 7,011 |
| 190 g/km | £73.50 | 29 | 9,377 | 9,002 | 8,656 | 8,336 | 8,038 | 7,761 | 7,502 | 7,260 | 7,033 |
| 195 g/km | £76.17 | 28 | 9,383 | 9,008 | 8,661 | 8,340 | 8,043 | 7,765 | 7,506 | 7,264 | 7,037 |
| 200 g/km | £78.67 | 27 | 9,345 | 8,971 | 8,626 | 8,307 | 8,010 | 7,734 | 7,476 | 7,235 | 7,009 |
| 205 g/km | £81.33 | 26 | 9,303 | 8,931 | 8,587 | 8,269 | 7,974 | 7,699 | 7,442 | 7,202 | 6,977 |
| 210 g/km | £84.00 | 25 | 9,239 | 8,869 | 8,528 | 8,212 | 7,919 | 7,646 | 7,391 | 7,153 | 6,929 |
| 215 g/km | £86.67 | 24 | 9,151 | 8,785 | 8,447 | 8,134 | 7,844 | 7,573 | 7,321 | 7,085 | 6,863 |
| 220 g/km | £89.33 | 23 | 9,039 | 8,678 | 8,344 | 8,035 | 7,748 | 7,481 | 7,231 | 6,998 | 6,779 |
| 225 g/km | £91.83 | 22 | 8,888 | 8,533 | 8,204 | 7,901 | 7,618 | 7,356 | 7,110 | 6,881 | 6,666 |

146

For example, if you drive a 160 g/km car and pay £1.35 per litre for petrol, you should pay the Fuel Scale Charge if you drive more than 7,893 private miles each year.

You can adjust for a different miles per gallon figure. For example, if you drive a 160 g/km car, pay £1.35 per litre for petrol and do 40 miles to the gallon, your minimum private mileage would be:

$$7,893 \times 40/35 = 9,021$$

Remember that the scale rates are subject to change if fuel prices significantly alter. Whether they will go down as quickly if fuel becomes cheaper is less certain! Remember also that the actual VAT savings involved may be very small, so as a rule of thumb it is probably only worth opting for the input tax restriction if your private mileage is say 50% of the figures in this table, given the extra work involved.

Now let's see what the figures are for diesel cars.

### Minimum Private Mileage for VAT Fuel Scale Rates (Diesel)

| CO2 Emissions | Quarterly Scale chg | Average MPG | Price of unleaded petrol per litre | | | | | | | | |
|---|---|---|---|---|---|---|---|---|---|---|---|
| | | | £1.27 | £1.32 | £1.37 | £1.42 | £1.47 | £1.52 | £1.57 | £1.62 | £1.67 |
| >120g/km | £26.17 | 65 | 7,071 | 6,803 | 6,555 | 6,324 | 6,109 | 5,908 | 5,720 | 5,543 | 5,378 |
| 125 g/km | £39.33 | 60 | 9,810 | 9,438 | 9,094 | 8,773 | 8,475 | 8,196 | 7,935 | 7,690 | 7,460 |
| 130 g/km | £42.00 | 55 | 9,603 | 9,239 | 8,902 | 8,588 | 8,296 | 8,023 | 7,768 | 7,528 | 7,303 |
| 135 g/km | £44.67 | 52 | 9,656 | 9,290 | 8,951 | 8,636 | 8,342 | 8,068 | 7,811 | 7,570 | 7,343 |
| 140 g/km | £47.17 | 51 | 10,000 | 9,622 | 9,270 | 8,944 | 8,640 | 8,356 | 8,089 | 7,840 | 7,605 |
| 145 g/km | £49.83 | 50 | 10,357 | 9,965 | 9,601 | 9,263 | 8,948 | 8,654 | 8,378 | 8,119 | 7,876 |
| 150 g/km | £52.50 | 48 | 10,476 | 10,079 | 9,711 | 9,369 | 9,050 | 8,753 | 8,474 | 8,212 | 7,966 |
| 155 g/km | £55.17 | 47 | 10,779 | 10,371 | 9,992 | 9,640 | 9,312 | 9,006 | 8,719 | 8,450 | 8,197 |
| 160 g/km | £57.67 | 46 | 11,028 | 10,610 | 10,223 | 9,863 | 9,527 | 9,214 | 8,921 | 8,645 | 8,386 |
| 165 g/km | £60.33 | 44 | 11,035 | 10,617 | 10,229 | 9,869 | 9,533 | 9,220 | 8,926 | 8,651 | 8,392 |
| 170 g/km | £63.00 | 43 | 11,261 | 10,835 | 10,439 | 10,072 | 9,729 | 9,409 | 9,109 | 8,828 | 8,564 |
| 175 g/km | £65.67 | 42 | 11,466 | 11,031 | 10,629 | 10,254 | 9,906 | 9,580 | 9,275 | 8,988 | 8,719 |
| 180 g/km | £68.17 | 40 | 11,335 | 10,906 | 10,508 | 10,138 | 9,793 | 9,471 | 9,169 | 8,886 | 8,620 |
| 185 g/km | £70.83 | 39 | 11,483 | 11,048 | 10,645 | 10,270 | 9,921 | 9,594 | 9,289 | 9,002 | 8,733 |
| 190 g/km | £73.50 | 38 | 11,610 | 11,171 | 10,763 | 10,384 | 10,031 | 9,701 | 9,392 | 9,102 | 8,830 |
| 195 g/km | £76.17 | 36 | 11,399 | 10,967 | 10,567 | 10,195 | 9,848 | 9,524 | 9,221 | 8,936 | 8,669 |
| 200 g/km | £78.67 | 35 | 11,446 | 11,012 | 10,611 | 10,237 | 9,889 | 9,563 | 9,259 | 8,973 | 8,704 |
| 205 g/km | £81.33 | 34 | 11,495 | 11,060 | 10,656 | 10,281 | 9,931 | 9,604 | 9,298 | 9,011 | 8,742 |
| 210 g/km | £84.00 | 33 | 11,523 | 11,087 | 10,682 | 10,306 | 9,955 | 9,628 | 9,321 | 9,034 | 8,763 |
| 215 g/km | £86.67 | 31 | 11,169 | 10,746 | 10,354 | 9,989 | 9,649 | 9,332 | 9,035 | 8,756 | 8,494 |
| 220 g/km | £89.33 | 30 | 11,140 | 10,718 | 10,327 | 9,964 | 9,625 | 9,308 | 9,012 | 8,733 | 8,472 |
| 225 g/km | £91.83 | 29 | 11,070 | 10,651 | 10,262 | 9,901 | 9,564 | 9,250 | 8,955 | 8,679 | 8,419 |

The parameters are the same in this table except that fuel prices are 7p higher and the MPG figures are about 30% higher.

You will note that the minimum mileage is significantly higher for diesel cars. That is because the scale charges are the same for both petrol and diesel cars even though the diesels have better fuel economy. If you drive a diesel car, you are more likely to pay excessive VAT if you pay the Fuel Scale Charge.

Finally, whichever method you use for claiming back VAT on fuel, always ask for a VAT receipt when you fill up and keep them somewhere safe (not screwed up in the back of the glove compartment). A VAT inspector will always ask to see them if you claim input tax on fuel or mileage, even if the amounts shown bear little resemblance to the amounts actually claimed.

# Chapter 12

# Decision # 5 - Should I Buy or Lease a Car for my Business?

This is a question worthy of a book all by itself!

Most of the answers have very little to do with tax. The buy or lease decision is normally driven by factors such as financing, running costs, maintenance contracts and corporate policy.

Many large corporations (and also private individuals) prefer to lease cars rather than buy them because they can avoid high depreciation charges, up-front capital commitments and ongoing administration costs, whilst benefiting from maintenance contracts that take care of servicing for a fixed monthly fee, thus avoiding unexpected cash outlays.

However, we need to focus on the tax issues, and for this purpose we will assume that the costs of buying and leasing are broadly the same over the life cycle of the car. Of course, this is not really true as it ignores the finance charges inherent within the lease rentals. However, it does enable us to directly compare the tax effects of buying and leasing cars.

Leasing cars differs from buying them in two major respects when it comes to tax:

- Income tax/corporation tax, and
- VAT

We will examine both sets of taxes as they affect cars, highlighting areas where the tax treatment is different. This may possibly enable you to gain a tax advantage.

# Tax Implications

We have already seen how capital allowances on cars are based on $CO_2$ emissions and this is something you need to take into account if you decide to buy a car for your business.

To recap: Cars with $CO_2$ emissions up to 110 g/km qualify for a 100% enhanced capital allowance.

Cars with $CO_2$ emissions between 111-160 g/km get writing-down allowances of 20% per annum (going down to 18% in April 2012).

Cars above 160 g/km only get writing-down allowances of 10% per annum (going down to 8% in April 2012).

However, a sole trader or partnership can claim a balancing allowance when a car is sold providing that:

- There is some private use by the proprietor or partners, and

- The car is not made available for the private use of their employees

Limited companies do not get balancing allowances on cars purchased on or after 1st April 2009 (there is a 5 year period of grace for cars purchased before that date).

But what happens if you lease the car instead? Well then it depends on whether it is a finance lease or an operating lease.

## *Finance Leases*

A finance lease is one where substantially all the risks and rewards of ownership belong to the lessee. This would normally be the case when an asset is leased for more than 90% of its useful economic life and the lessee can acquire the asset at the end of the lease term for a notional fee. A typical example would be an aeroplane leased by an airline.

With a finance lease the lessee is entitled to claim capital allowances as though it actually owned the asset. The tax treatment recognises the economic substance of the contract rather than its legal form.

## Operating Leases

An operating lease is where substantially all the risks and rewards of ownership remain with the lessor. This normally happens when the lease period is 3-5 years and the lessee has to pay a market value price to acquire the asset at the end of the lease term, should it wish to do so. Car leases are normally treated as operating leases.

With an operating lease, no capital allowances can be claimed by the lessee. Instead, the lease payments are treated as running costs and expensed through the profit and loss account.

## Tax Advantages of Leasing

Given the fact that capital allowances are quite low now on most cars and limited companies cannot claim balancing allowances when a car is sold, you might think that there is a tax advantage in leasing cars given that the rentals can be claimed against tax as and when they arise.

Indeed this is true but with one important qualification: If the $CO_2$ emissions of leased cars exceed 160 g/km and the car has been leased since 6th April 2009 (or 1st April 2009 for companies), you must disallow 15% of the lease rentals against tax. Otherwise, the lease rentals are allowable in full.

For cars leased before 6th April 2009 (or 1st April 2009 for companies) the position is more complicated. For those cars, lease rentals are only allowable in full if the list price was £12,000 or less.

Otherwise you must disallow 50% of the lease rentals on the proportion of the list price exceeding £12,000. For example, if a car with a list price of £20,000 is leased for £300 a month, you must disallow £300 x 8/20 x 50% per month.

You can see from this that the income tax/corporation tax position is therefore affected by two factors:

- The capital allowances available on purchased cars, and
- The lease rentals deductible on leased cars

Both of these factors are determined by the car's $CO_2$ emissions.

151

## Case Studies 7.1 to 7.5

The following case studies look at whether it is better to lease or buy depending on the $CO_2$ emissions of your car and whether you trade through a limited company or not.

### Case Study # 7.1

On 6th April 2011 Alpha LLP takes delivery of a new car with $CO_2$ emissions of 160 g/km and must decide whether to buy it for £20,000 or lease it for three years at £400 a month. If it buys the car it will incur finance costs of £1,400 but can sell it after 3 years for £7,000. If it leases the car it will have an option to buy it after 3 years for £7,000. The partners pay tax at 40% and have 30% private use of the car. Ignore the time value of money. What is the most tax efficient option?

| Buying | |
|---|---|
| Purchase cost – 2011/12 | +£20,000 |
| Capital allowance – 2011/12<br>£20,000 x 20% x 70% business use x 40% income tax | -£1,120 |
| Capital allowance – 2012/13<br>£16,000 x 18% x 70% business use x 40% income tax | -£806 |
| Capital allowance – 2013/14<br>£13,120 x 18% x 70% x 40% | -£661 |
| Disposal proceeds – 2014/15 | -£7,000 |
| Balancing allowance – 2014/15<br>(£13,000 x 70% - £6,468*) x 40% | -£1,053 |
| Finance cost | +£1,400 |
| Tax saved on Finance cost - £1,400 x 40% | -£560 |
| Acquisition cost net of tax | +£10,200 |
| | |
| **Leasing** | |
| Monthly rentals - £400 x 36 | +£14,400 |
| Tax saved on lease rentals<br>£14,400 x 70% x 40% | -£4,032 |
| Acquisition cost net of tax | +£10,368 |
| | |
| **Additional benefit of buying** | **+£168** |

\* £6,468 = (£1,120 + £806 + £661) / 40%

The first thing to note about this example is that it involves a partnership rather than a limited company, so if the car was bought there should be a balancing allowance on disposal.

The non-tax cash flows have been made exactly the same with both options (which is unlikely to happen in reality).

Furthermore, the $CO_2$ emissions do not exceed 160 g/km so the lease rentals are 100% tax deductible.

Given the equality of the cash flows, you might expect the tax effects to be the same with both options, but they are not as buying the car gives you an extra £168 tax relief.

This is due to the tax treatment of the finance cost. If there was a finance deal on the car, the interest would have to be restricted by 30% for private use the same as the lease rentals.

But if the finance cost represented interest foregone on a deposit account or interest payable on an overdraft or a general loan for the business itself, then it would be 100% deductible against tax as it is not specific to the car.

We have assumed in this example that the finance cost is not specific, so the £168 represents 30% of £1,400 x 40%.

## Case Study # 7.2

Now we will look at the same example again except that this time $CO_2$ emissions exceed 160 g/km. Therefore, only 85% of the lease rentals (before the private use restriction) are tax deductible.

| Buying | |
|---|---|
| Purchase cost – 2011/12 | +£20,000 |
| Capital allowance – 2011/12<br>£20,000 x 10% x 70% business use x 40% income tax | -£560 |
| Capital allowance – 2012/13<br>£18,000 x 8% x 70% business use x 40% income tax | -£403 |
| Capital allowance – 2013/14<br>£16,560 x 8% x 70% x 40% | -£371 |
| Disposal proceeds – 2014/15 | -£7,000 |
| Balancing allowance – 2014/15<br>(£13,000 x 70% - £3,335*) x 40% | -£2,306 |
| Finance cost | +£1,400 |
| Tax saved on finance cost - £1,400 x 40% | -£560 |
| Acquisition cost net of tax | +£10,200 |
| | |
| **Leasing** | |
| Monthly rentals - £400 x 36 | +£14,400 |
| Tax saved on lease rentals<br>£14,400 x 85% x 70% x 40% | -£3,427 |
| Acquisition cost net of tax | +£10,973 |
| | |
| **Additional benefit of buying** | **+£773** |

* £3,335 = (£560 + £403 + £371) / 40%

Here we can see that it is better to buy the car due to the 15% disallowance of the lease rentals. There is no equivalent restriction on capital allowances if Alpha LLP was to buy the car.

The balancing allowance on disposal makes it advantageous for the partnership to buy the car. In this example, the additional benefit of £773 less the £168 already identified in the previous example equals £605.

This represents lease rentals of £14,400 x 15% x 70% x 40%.

## Case Study # 7.3

For a limited company the position is more complex since the company cannot claim a balancing allowance on disposal. The following example is based on the same facts as Case Study # 7.1 except that Alpha is a limited company so there is no balancing allowance when it sells the car and there is no private use restriction. Also, the corporation tax rate is only 20%.

| Buying | |
|---|---:|
| Purchase cost – 2011/12 | +£20,000 |
| Capital allowance – 2011/12 £20,000 x 20% x 20% | -£800 |
| Capital allowance – 2012/13 £16,000 x 18% x 20% | -£576 |
| Capital allowance – 2013/14 £13,120 x 18% x 20% | -£472 |
| Disposal proceeds – 2014/15 | -£7,000 |
| Finance cost | +£1,400 |
| Tax saved on finance cost - £1,400 x 20% | -£280 |
| Acquisition cost net of tax | +£12,272 |
| | |
| **Leasing** | |
| Monthly rentals - £400 x 36 | +£14,400 |
| Tax saved on lease rentals - £14,400 x 20% | -£2,880 |
| Acquisition cost net of tax | +£11,520 |
| | |
| **Additional benefit of leasing** | **+£752** |

Now it is better for Alpha Limited to lease the car. The net cost of the car is £13,000 but Alpha will only get capital allowances of £9,240 up to the disposal date. It will get the remaining £3,760 eventually and save tax on this at whatever the corporation tax rate happens to be in future, but it would take many years. Inflation would quickly erode the benefit of this tax relief.

Note that we have not factored in the tax and national insurance payable on the car benefit. This is because it would be the same whether the car is bought or leased, so is irrelevant to the decision.

## Case Study # 7.4

Suppose $CO_2$ emissions were higher than 160 g/km? What should Alpha Limited do then? We know that capital allowances would be even lower, but lease rentals would suffer a 15% restriction, so which would harm the company most?

| Buying | |
|---|---|
| Purchase cost – 2011/12 | +£20,000 |
| Capital allowance – 2011/12 £20,000 x 10% x 20% | -£400 |
| Capital allowance – 2012/13 £18,000 x 8% x 20% | -£288 |
| Capital allowance – 2013/14 £16,560 x 8% x 20% | -£265 |
| Disposal proceeds – 2014/15 | -£7,000 |
| Finance cost | +£1,400 |
| Tax saved on finance cost – £1,400 x 20% | -£280 |
| Acquisition cost net of tax | +£13,167 |
| | |
| **Leasing** | |
| Monthly rentals - £400 x 36 | +£14,400 |
| Tax saved on lease rentals - £14,400 x 85% x 20% | -£2,448 |
| Acquisition cost net of tax | +£11,952 |
| | |
| **Additional benefit of leasing** | **+£1,215** |

We can see that leasing becomes even more attractive. Tax relief on the lease rentals goes down by £432 but capital allowances go down by £895. Consequently, the benefit of leasing goes up by £463 (£1,215 less £752).

In a fantasy world of zero inflation, zero finance costs and unlimited life spans, it would eventually be better to buy as the company would finally obtain all remaining capital allowances after about 30-40 years.

In the real world, however, inflation would probably have doubled or trebled the cost of living by then, and the owners of the company are likely to have either retired or died, so from a tax point of view it would undoubtedly be better to lease.

*Case Study # 7.5*

Of course, if $CO_2$ emissions were no higher than 110 g/km Alpha Limited would not need to worry about this as it would obtain a 100% capital allowance on buying the car. True, it would have to pay back some of this when the car was sold, but would still obtain full tax relief on the net cost.

As the lease rentals would also be allowable in full, there should be no difference from a tax point of view between buying and leasing. The next example proves that this is indeed true.

| Buying | |
|---|---|
| Purchase cost – 2011/12 | +£20,000 |
| Capital allowance – 2011/12 £20,000 x 100% x 20% | -£4,000 |
| Disposal proceeds – 2014/15 | -£7,000 |
| Balancing charge – 2014/15 £7,000 x 20% | +£1,400 |
| Finance cost | +£1,400 |
| Tax saved on finance cost - £1,400 x 20% | -£280 |
| Acquisition cost net of tax | +£11,520 |
| | |
| **Leasing** | |
| Monthly rentals - £400 x 36 | +£14,400 |
| Tax saved on lease rentals - £14,400 x 20% | -£2,880 |
| Acquisition cost net of tax | +£11,520 |
| | |
| **Additional benefit of leasing** | **£0** |

## VAT Effects

All the above examples exclude VAT and assume that Alpha is not VAT registered. However, if the business *is* VAT registered, then this can make a huge difference to the buy or lease decision. The reason for that is that VAT generally cannot be reclaimed on the purchase price of cars. Unless the car is used 100% for business with no private use whatsoever (which would be very difficult to prove) no VAT can be claimed on the purchase price.

In fact, HM Revenue & Customs may challenge any VAT recovery on principle unless it was an obvious exemption, e.g. a taxi.

Leased cars enjoy an advantage as the lessee is able to recover 50% of the VAT on the lease rentals, provided there is **some** business use. To understand the impact this might have on the buy/lease decision, the following example is based on the same facts as Case Study 7.1 but this time on the basis that Alpha is VAT registered.

### Case Study # 7.6

On 6th April 2011 Alpha LLP takes delivery of a new car with $CO_2$ emissions of 160 g/km and must decide whether to buy it for £20,000 or lease it for 3 years at £400 a month. If it buys the car finance costs will be £1,400 but it can be sold after 3 years for £7,000. If it leases the car it will have an option to buy after 3 years for £7,000. The partners pay tax at 40% and have 30% private use of the car. Ignore the time value of money. What is the most tax efficient option?

| **Buying** | |
| --- | --- |
| Purchase cost – 2011/12 | +£20,000 |
| Capital allowance – 2011/12 £20,000 x 20% x 70% x 40% | -£1,120 |
| Capital allowance – 2012/13 £16,000 x 18% x 70% x 40% | -£806 |
| Capital allowance – 2013/14 £13,120 x 18% x 70% x 40% | -£661 |
| Disposal proceeds – 2014/15 | -£7,000 |
| Balancing allowance – 2014/15 13,000 x 70% - £6,468 x 40% | -£1,053 |
| Finance cost | +£1,400 |
| Tax saved on finance cost - £1,400 x 40% | -£560 |
| Acquisition cost net of tax | +£10,200 |
| | |
| **Leasing** | |
| Monthly rentals - £400 x 36 | +£14,400 |
| Tax saved on lease rentals £14,400 x 70% x 40% | -£4,032 |
| VAT saved on lease rentals £14,400 x 20/120 x 50% | -£1,200 |
| Acquisition cost net of tax | +£9,168 |
| | |
| **Additional benefit of leasing** | **+£1,032** |

We can see that there is now a big advantage in leasing rather than buying. The VAT recovery makes a huge difference. It is also worth noting that VAT ought to be lower in the first place for leased cars as the cost of the lease will be based on the residual value of the car, whereas for cars that are purchased new it will be based on the market value.

You will note that capital allowances in the above example have not been reduced by the VAT element. That is because they can usually be claimed on the whole cost of the car, including VAT, whether the buyer is VAT registered or not. It is only if the buyer is able to recover VAT on the purchase price, say for a pool car or a taxi, that VAT must be excluded from the amount claimed for capital allowances.

## Summary

From these examples, we can now draw the following conclusions for the buy/lease decision:

- VAT-registered businesses are normally better off leasing cars rather than buying them.

- Limited companies are normally better off leasing cars due to the absence of balancing allowances.

- Sole traders and partnerships may be better of buying cars if $CO_2$ emissions exceed 160 g/km.

- Tax relief on the finance cost may be decisive where all other tax considerations are neutral.

However, we must repeat the warning we have made all the way through this book: Never let the tax tail wag the investment dog. This is especially true with the buy/lease decision as there are so many other factors that may be relevant.

In particular, it is highly unlikely that the various non-tax cash flows are going to be conveniently neutral as shown in our examples. For example, the finance charges implicit within lease rentals are normally higher than the finance costs associated with buying a car.

159

# Chapter 13

# Decision # 6
# What Type of Car is Best for My Business?

As mentioned at the very start of this book, this is a question that depends largely on your own personal likes and dislikes. Tax is just one of many considerations, albeit an important one for business owners. Notwithstanding this, there are some general points we can make that may assist in this decision.

## Limited Companies

If you run your business through a limited company and choose to have a company car, you will be treated as an ordinary employee as far as the taxman is concerned and pay income tax on a car benefit in kind. Not only that, but your company will pay Class 1A national insurance contributions at 13.8%.

Obviously it is in your interests to minimise these taxes as much as possible. The most obvious advice is therefore to choose a car with low $CO_2$ emissions or a low list price, preferably both.

It will not help you to buy second hand as you will be taxed on the original list price, regardless of how much you pay for the car.

You will also want to buy cars that tend to hold their value well in order to claim as much of the net cost as possible in capital allowances before the car is sold. This tends to point towards a policy of buying cars new and replacing them every 2-3 years.

For a company, the golden rule is to avoid cars with $CO_2$ emissions above 160 g/km. The capital allowances are much lower (only 8% per year from April 2012). If the car is leased, 15% of the monthly rentals would be disallowed.

## Sole Traders and Partnerships

For the self-employed who do not work through their own limited companies (or give cars to their staff) there is no need to worry about income tax on a car benefit in kind.

The only consideration is how to maximise their capital allowances or tax relief on lease rentals. As sole traders and partners are still able to claim a balancing allowance when they sell their cars, ultimately they will obtain full tax relief on the net capital cost anyway.

This is extremely tax efficient for those who like to change their cars every few years and upgrade to bigger and better models. In effect, it advances the tax relief on the net capital cost of the car, even if capital allowances are only 8% per annum.

However, you would need to do fairly high business mileage to make the most of capital allowances because you must reduce the capital allowance by the private use proportion.

It is also more worthwhile for sole traders and partners to purchase second hand cars, as they are not taxed on the original list price. They will also avoid VAT as most second-hand cars are sold exclusive of VAT.

## Electric Cars

Electric cars are worth knowing about because there is no tax on them at all, including Vehicle Excise Duty and the London Congestion Charge.

At the time of writing, however, it is still early days in the electric cars revolution and they are not yet a viable solution for many drivers. This is mainly because they are still relatively expensive, there is only a small product range and, more importantly, charging points are still few and far between. Electric cars are probably best for driving around major cities where there are more charging points and the stored energy will last longer.

The Greater London Authority is aiming to have 7,500 charge points in London by Spring 2013 and 25,000 by 2015. The aim is to have at least 100,000 electric cars in London by the year 2020.

By May 2011 there were already 17,000 hybrid and pure electric vehicles on the road in Greater London. There is also now a network of charging points run by an organisation called Source London, which you can join for £100 a year. The charge points are accessible by the public in supermarkets, public car parks, shopping and leisure centres and residential streets. You can also use charge points run by London boroughs.

Most electric cars currently available have a range of less than 100 miles. If you use your car every day, you will probably need to charge it every 2-3 days. How long does it take to charge an electric car? That depends on the type of vehicle you own, the type of charge-point you use and whether you want a full charge or just a top-up. According to the Source London website (www.sourcelondon.net/charge-points) the time taken for a full charge is as follows:

|  | **Cars** | **Small Vans** | **Large Vans and Trucks** |
|---|---|---|---|
| Standard point | 5-8 hours | 6-8 hours | > 8 hours |
| Fast point | 3-4 hours | 3-4 hours | 4-8 hours |
| Rapid point | < 30 mins | < 30 mins | > 1 hour |

Charging probably takes longer and is required more frequently than you might have expected (or be prepared to put up with). Also, unless you are prepared to stand by your car and wait a few hours or just do a quick (30 minute) top-up, you will probably need to leave your car unattended at the charge point.

Fortunately, it is possible to charge your own vehicle at home or work. You don't have to go to a public charging point. In fact, you don't have to use a charging point at all as most electric cars can be charged from an ordinary domestic wall socket.

However, it would be necessary to have off-street parking in order to charge your car from a household supply.

Charge-posts for private use cost around £500 plus VAT, fitting and delivery. However, a growing number of companies are now offering these products and one would expect the price to come down a fair bit over the next few years.

# Chapter 14

# Decision # 7

# Should I Take a Cash Alternative?

So far we've only looked at company cars from a business owner's point of view. For a regular employee, the decision will be based on quite different factors.

Obviously employees will be unconcerned about capital allowances, employer national insurance or corporation tax. For them, the decision will boil down to one question at the end of the day – will the income tax on a company car be higher or lower than the cost of buying and running a car themselves?

## Relevant Factors

If you are offered a company car by your employer, the financial benefit will depend on the following factors:

- The income tax charge on the car
- The cost of buying the car
- The cost of running the car
- How long you keep the car
- How much business mileage you do
- How much you get for business mileage
- The latest advisory fuel rates
- How much you spend on fuel
- Personal contributions for the car
- Your highest income tax rate
- The employee national insurance rate
- Your own cost of capital
- The type of car you want to drive

Let's look at each of these factors in turn.

### The income tax charge on the car

The taxable benefit-in-kind charge on a company car is based on two things: the original list price and the taxable percentage.

The list price never changes but the taxable percentages usually go up each year. They range from 10% to 35%, depending on the car's $CO_2$ emissions and the type of fuel it runs on.

Diesels are subject to an additional 3% but with a 35% maximum. For road fuel gas you can use the list price of an equivalent car that runs on petrol.

### The cost of buying the car

You must compare like with like here. Obviously it is no use comparing a brand new BMW with a second-hand Ford Fiesta. The comparison will only work if the car is identical on both sides of the equation, including the year of registration. Of course, your employer may well be able to buy the car cheaper than you due to bulk discounts, but that is not relevant. All that matters is how much an identical car is going to cost you.

### The costs of running the car

Obviously if you own the car personally you will be responsible for all the running costs, such as insurance, maintenance, road tax and breakdown cover. As an employee you cannot claim any of these costs against tax, whereas your employer can. However, you may be able to run the car much cheaper than your employer.

For example, your employer may have its cars serviced by a main dealer, whilst you would be happy to take it to Joe's Autos down the road. Similarly, your motor insurance may be cheaper if you shop around a bit. This should be factored into your decision.

However, in the case of maintenance, you should consider the risk of invalidating your warranty if you do not have the car serviced by a main dealer and it is damaged as a result. You may also find motor insurance much more expensive than your employer, pay an excess if you make a claim on your policy and incur extra costs such as hire cars or accident recovery.

### How long you will keep the car

This is important because it will affect the annual depreciation charge. Generally, the longer you keep a car the cheaper it will be, as the original cost less the eventual sale proceeds will be spread over more years. However, the tax charge on a company car will remain more or less the same each year (apart from changes to the taxable percentages).

If you are happy to keep a car for 6 years, you can compare the average annual cost with the tax charge on a company car even if your employer would have replaced it after 4 years. Obviously there would be a difference in terms of quality between cars of different ages so you would not exactly be comparing like for like, but if you are happy to run an older car for a couple of years you are perfectly entitled to bring this into the equation.

### How much business mileage you do

If you use your own car for business journeys you will be entitled to claim mileage expenses from your employer. This may reduce your costs of running the car quite substantially. We must assume here that, if you had a company car, you would reimburse all private mileage according to the latest advisory fuel rates, or pay for all fuel up front and claim expenses from your employer for business mileage. If you drive many business miles, you may be better off owning the car yourself rather than paying tax on a car with relatively little private use.

### How much you get for business mileage

This depends on how generous your employer is. If you own the car yourself, you can claim business mileage tax free up to 45p per mile for the first 10,000 miles during the tax year and 25p for all additional miles. You can also claim an extra 5p per mile for any passengers you take with you on company business.

These rates are not particularly generous now as they have not kept pace with inflation over the last 10 years. Also, they are meant to cover all motoring costs, not just fuel. Nevertheless your employer may reimburse less than this to you, in which case you would be entitled to claim the shortfall against tax.

## *The latest advisory fuel rates*

If you drive a company car and pay for all fuel yourself, you can claim for business mileage at the latest advisory fuel rates. If your employer reimburses more than this you could get taxed on an £18,800 private fuel benefit, unless you can prove the actual fuel costs were at least as high as the amount reimbursed. Usually it would be quite difficult to do this though. They may be called advisory, but as far as the taxman is concerned they are more or less compulsory.

You can look up the latest advisory fuel rates at:

www.hmrc.gov.uk/cars/advisory_fuel_current.htm

They are meant to reflect the prices at the pumps and are updated regularly. However, this will usually only be once a quarter, so if fuel prices are rocketing due to instability in the Middle East or industrial disputes they may temporarily be on the low side.

This will benefit you if your employer pays for all fuel and you are required to reimburse them for private mileage, but if you pay for all fuel yourself and then claim expenses for business mileage at the advisory rates, you could lose out.

There is supposed to be a mechanism built into the system whereby the advisory fuel rates are updated early if prices at the pumps rise more than 5%. However, HM Revenue & Customs only seems to invoke this when nagged into doing so by the fleet operators via their representative body ACFO.

## *How much you spend on fuel*

It follows from this that if you do a lot of mileage in your company car the effect of any short-term disparities in the advisory fuel rates will be magnified. So will any disparities caused by the fuel efficiency of your car or the price of fuel locally.

For example, if you fill up regularly at motorway service stations, you can expect to pay more for fuel than you can claim back from your employer. On the other hand, you may get discounts off your fuel bills by using coupons from the supermarket.

## Personal contributions for the car

Personal contributions are amounts paid by the employee to their employer towards a company car. There are two types of contribution you can make – capital contributions and private use contributions. The detailed rules were explained in Chapter 2 so will not be repeated here.

Private use contributions will not reduce your overall cost because a higher-rate taxpayer would have to pay £1 just to save 40p. They will simply increase the cost to you of having a company car.

Capital contributions, on the other hand, may reduce the cost of a company car in the long run if you are a higher-rate taxpayer and keep the car for several years, as they will reduce the list price (and hence the tax charge) for **each** year that you drive the car. You would also be entitled to a partial rebate when the car is sold.

## Your highest income tax rate

If you are a higher-rate taxpayer you will obviously pay twice as much tax on your company car at 40% than a basic-rate taxpayer would at 20%. If you take a cash alternative instead, this will also be taxed at your top rate. However, it may be higher or lower than the company car taxable benefit, so your tax bill may change.

## Employee NI rate

Company car users do not pay employee national insurance on the benefit-in-kind charge. However, if you take a cash alternative instead, that would be subject to employee national insurance as part of your salary. Employee national insurance is only 2% for higher-rate taxpayers but 12% for basic-rate taxpayers, so for lower paid workers it makes much more difference.

## Your own cost of capital

If you need to borrow money to buy a car yourself, the interest you pay must be taken into account. Even if you do not need to borrow, there will usually be an opportunity cost such as the interest foregone in a savings account.

### *The type of car you want to drive*

This is more of a qualitative factor and not easily brought into the calculations. If you are entitled to a company car superior to one you could afford yourself and you enjoy driving that car, you would simply work out how much it would cost you to buy and run that car personally. However, if you are not really bothered about driving a superior car but your employer tells you that you must have one anyway (to maintain the company image perhaps), you may view the tax charge on it as an unnecessary expense.

On the other side of the coin, perhaps your employer can only offer you a mediocre car as a workhorse when you would prefer to drive a superior car. Then you would have to take into account the fact that you are compromising on quality.

A few case studies should make it clear when it is financially beneficial for you to have a company car from your employer and when it might perhaps be better to accept a cash alternative instead. We are going to assume here that the employee earns more than £8,500 per year (including the company car benefit). So-called 'lower-paid employees' who earn less than this are exempt from tax on benefits but are a very rare species these days.

## Case Study # 8.1 - Green Car

Max is a salesman for Pest-Call Windows Ltd and drives a company car with a list price of £15,000 and $CO_2$ emissions of 117 g/km. It has a 1600cc engine and runs on diesel. Max drives 20,000 miles a year of which 15,000 are for business. He uses a corporate card to pay for all fuel and reimburses his employer for private mileage at an advisory fuel rate of 12p per mile. He is not required to pay contributions towards private use of the car.

Max wonders if he would be better off owning the car himself and taking a cash alternative instead. If he bought the car himself, it would cost him £14,500 and he would have to take out a loan for 4 years at an average rate of 5%. At the end of the 4 years he would sell the car for £5,000 and pay off the loan. He pays £1.42 per litre for fuel and his fuel consumption is 6 miles per litre. His employer reimburses business mileage for staff using their own cars at 25p per mile. His other running costs would be £2,000 per annum.

Max earns £25,000 a year and has taxable investment income of £3,000. His personal allowance is £7,475 and the higher-rate tax band starts at £35,000 (on taxable income). He makes no pension contributions or gift aid donations and there is nothing else that would affect his tax. Basic-rate tax is 20% and higher-rate tax is 40%. How much better off is he with a company car?

### Solution

First we must look at how all this data affects his financial position. Income tax is clearly the main cost to Max for a company car. A car with $CO_2$ emissions of 117 g/km qualifies for the 10% band in 2011/12 but on 6th April 2012 the rate jumps to 14%.

As it is a diesel Max is taxed on an extra 3%. We will assume that the rates for the next 2 years are unchanged. The average rate over the 4 years is therefore 16%. The list price is £15,000 so Max will have a taxable benefit of £1,950 in 2011/12 and £2,550 for the next 3 years (we must compare both options over the same period of time so 4 years altogether).

### Working 1

How much tax will Max pay on the car? His salary is £25,000 and the car benefit in kind (BIK) is £2,550 from 2012 onwards. His investment income is £3,000 so his total income for the year is £30,550. He is well below the higher-rate threshold so he is a basic-rate taxpayer. The company car benefit will be taxed at 20% and none of his investment income will be pushed into the higher-rate tax bracket. His total tax bill over the 4 years will therefore be:

£1,950 BIK x 20% + £2,550 BIK x 20% x 3 = **£1,920**.

### Working 2

Then there is fuel. His employer pays for this on the corporate card but Max must reimburse private mileage. He drives 20,000 miles a year and 15,000 are for business, so private mileage is 5,000.

The advisory fuel rate for a diesel car up to 1600cc is 12p per mile at present, so he must pay at least £600 per year to avoid paying tax on a fuel benefit, which adds up to **£2,400** over the 4 years.

## *Working 3*

Now we must consider his costs for running his own car. First there is the purchase price of £14,500 less the re-sale value of £5,000 so that is a net cost of **£9,500** over the 4 years.

We will ignore the time value of money in this example, although you should factor this in if inflation or interest rates are particularly high.

## *Working 4*

The average balance on the loan over the 4 years would be £9,750 (£14,500 + £5,000) x 50%. Total interest would therefore be:

$$£9,750 \text{ x } 5\% \text{ x } 4 \text{ years} = £1,950.$$

## *Working 5*

Fuel costs will be £4,733 per annum, being 20,000 miles divided by the consumption rate of 6 miles per litre, multiplied by the price per litre of £1.42. Over 4 years this would come to **£18,933**.

In reality, of course, fuel prices will change all the time, but we can safely assume the advisory fuel rates will too. Not so the 45p/25p approved mileage rates for people using their own cars. They may well be frozen for the foreseeable future.

In fact, the main rate of 40p was frozen for 9 years from 6th April 2002 to 5th April 2011, and the 25p rate has never been increased at all, so you can just imagine how much the value of these rates has eroded against the price of fuel and other running costs.

## Working 6

Max can only claim 25p per mile for business use from his employer anyway, so he will recover **£15,000** (being 15,000 miles x 25p x 4 years).

That may seem like a good result given that it is only £3,933 less than his total fuel bills but of course the mileage rates are meant to cover his depreciation and running costs too.

## Working 7

Max can get a tax rebate for the shortfall on the tax-free mileage rates. If his employer reimbursed business mileage at the 45p/25p rates, he would have received £5,750 per annum (being 10,000 x 45p + 5,000 x 25p). That comes to £23,000 over 4 years.

In fact he will only get £15,000 so he can claim £8,000 against tax. At 20% that will give him total tax rebates of **£1,600**.

## Working 8

The other running costs will be £2,000 a year so **£8,000** in total. In practice it is these that make all the difference. If you can keep these down you might well be better off with extra salary instead of a company car.

Of course, insurance is usually the largest and most unpredictable one. This will depend mainly on your age, sex, car, address, claims record and driving history. If you can't get a good deal on your insurance you may well be better off with a company car, assuming your employer does not make you pay for your cover under their fleet policy!

Let's put all these numbers together and see how it works out for Max.

## Cost of Company Car

| | | |
|---|---|---|
| Tax on benefit | *Working 1* | +£1,920 |
| Private mileage | *Working 2* | +£2,400 |
| Total costs | | +£4,320 |

## Cost of Own Car

| | | |
|---|---|---|
| Purchase cost less sale proceeds | *Working 3* | +£9,500 |
| Interest on loan | *Working 4* | +£1,950 |
| Total fuel costs | *Working 5* | +£18,933 |
| Less: Mileage claims | *Working 6* | -£15,000 |
| Less: Tax rebates on business mileage | *Working 7* | -£1,600 |
| Other running costs | *Working 8* | +£8,000 |
| Total costs | | +£21,783 |

**Additional cost of own car over 4 years**      **+£17,463**

**Additional cost pa**      **+£4,366**

So Max would need an extra £4,366 per annum to be in the same financial position as he would with a company car. Of course, that is after tax and national insurance. How much would his cash alternative need to be? As a basic-rate taxpayer, he would need to gross up this figure by 68% to £6,420. He would then be left with £4,366 after his employer deducts 20% income tax and 12% national insurance.

Is he likely to get this much? It depends on how much money his employer can save by *not* giving him a company car. This in turn depends on its marginal rate of corporation tax. A large company will pay tax at 26% in 2011/12. A small company will pay 20% and those making profits between £300,000 and £1.5 million will pay a marginal rate of 27.5%.

Let's assume the employer is a large company and its marginal corporation tax rate is 26% in 2011/12, reducing by 1% a year to 23% in 2014/15. How much will they save by offering the employee extra salary instead of a car?

## Working 9

The employer will save first on the purchase cost of the car. Let's assume they could have bought this cheaper than Max at £14,000. They would have sold it after four years for £5,000 so that's a net saving of £9,000. The capital allowance would have been worth 18% per annum on the written-down value (apart from the first year when the writing-down allowance is 20%). After 4 years they would have claimed back 77% of the net cost which is £6,930. The corporation tax saving at 23%-26% would have been £1,734 so overall their net purchase cost after tax will be **£7,266**.

## Working 10

The employer will also save Class 1A national insurance on the benefit. We have already calculated the benefit as £1,950 in 2011/12 and £2,550 over the next 3 years. At 13.8% that would have cost them £269 in Year 1 and £352 in Years 2-4. Deduct tax savings at 26% in Year 1 and an average 24% in Years 2-4 and their net saving is **£1,002**.

## Working 11

They will pay Max £15,000 for business mileage at 25p per mile. On a company car they would have paid £18,933 but recovered £2,400 from Max for private mileage, so their net cost would have been £16,533. We'll ignore VAT as that would have been the same either way (assuming they do not use the scale rates for output tax). They therefore save £1,533 extra on fuel/mileage which is **£1,157** after deducting tax at an average 24.5%

## Working 12

Let's now assume they save running costs of £3,000 per annum of which £1,500 includes VAT. This is £1,000 a year more than Max would pay but assumes they use a main dealer for servicing and incur administration overheads too. Over 4 years they would save £11,000 (being £12,000 less £1,000 VAT recoveries). Deduct corporation tax at an average rate of 24.5% and their net saving is **£8,305**.

## Working 13

We should also factor in their cost of capital. To compare like with like, we'll assume this only arises on the net purchase cost as with Max. We'll be generous and assume they can achieve 5% per annum on the net cash flow of £9,000 (on the basis that the sale proceeds on old cars are re-invested each year). That will give them extra income of £450 per annum or £1,800 over 4 years. Deduct tax at an average 24.5% and the net amount is **£1,359**.

So the overall saving for the employer will be as follows:

| | | |
|---|---|---|
| Net cost of car | *Working 9* | +£7,266 |
| Employer NI | *Working 10* | +£1,002 |
| Fuel/mileage costs | *Working 11* | +£1,157 |
| Other running costs (net of VAT) | *Working 12* | +£8,305 |
| Cost of capital | *Working 13* | +£1,359 |
| **Total savings over 4 years** | | **+£19,089** |
| **Total saving per annum** | | **+£4,772** |

If the employer pays Max a cash alternative of £6,420 per annum they will have to pay employer national insurance of 13.8% but save corporation tax at an average 24.5%. Their net cost after tax would therefore be £5,516. So it looks like Max will be disappointed. His employer cannot afford to pay him as much as he needs to run his own car as they would lose £744 a year.

At most the employer would be able to pay Max a cash alternative of £5,554 per annum. This would be worth £3,777 to Max after tax and national insurance, leaving him £589 a year worse off. Max will therefore be better off keeping his company car rather than joining the so-called *grey fleet*.

It should be borne in mind that Working 9 only includes 77% of the capital allowance as that is all that has been earned after 4 years. In practice, the employer will earn the remaining 23% over the next 20 years, although 90% will have been earned by Year 8. Therefore, the employer could afford to increase the Cash Alternative slightly to reflect this, but not by enough to affect the overall outcome.

We have also assumed that the employer does not lease the car and claim back 50% of the VAT on the rentals, which they could have passed on to Max. We will address this particular aspect later.

Let's try another example – this time assuming a higher-rate taxpayer with a more expensive car.

## Case Study # 8.2 – Gas Guzzler

Rupert is a director of Big Bonus Bank Ltd and drives a company car with a list price of £32,000 and $CO_2$ emissions of 225 g/km. It has a 2500cc engine and runs on petrol. Rupert drives 10,000 miles a year of which 1,000 are for business. He pays for all fuel himself and claims business mileage from his employer at an advisory fuel rate of 26p per mile. He is required to pay contributions of £50 per month towards private use of the car.

Rupert wonders if he would be better off owning the car himself and taking a cash alternative instead. If he bought the car himself, it would cost him £30,000 and he would have to take out a loan for 4 years at an average rate of 5%. At the end of the 4 years he would sell the car for £8,000 and pay off the balance of the loan.

He pays £1.35 per litre for fuel and his fuel consumption is 4 miles per litre. The bank reimburses employees for business mileage in their own cars at 30p per mile. His other running costs would be £4,000 per annum.

Rupert earns a salary of £250,000 a year and pays tax at a top rate of 50%. Big Bonus Bank Ltd pays corporation tax at 23-26% over the 4 years and recovers no VAT as all its supplies are exempt. Is Rupert better off with a company car?

### *Solution*

### *Working 1*

The tax charge would be 35% of list price for all 4 years. The total taxable benefit over the 4 years will therefore be £44,800 less private use contributions of £2,400 and Rupert will pay 50% tax of **£21,200.**

175

### Working 2

Total fuel costs are 10,000 miles x £1.35/4 miles/litre x 4 years = £13,500. The bank reimburses 1,000 miles x 26p x 4 years = £1,040. Net fuel costs are therefore **£12,460**.

### Working 3

Private use contributions are £50 x 12 months x 4 years = **£2,400**.

### Working 4

The net cost if Rupert bought the car himself would be £30,000 less £8,000 sales proceeds = **£22,000**.

### Working 5

The average balance on his loan would be (£30,000 + £8,000) x 50% = £19,000. Interest at 5% per annum over 4 years would be **£3,800**.

### Working 6

Total fuel costs are £13,500 as per Working 2. The bank reimburses 1,000 miles x 30p x 4 years = £1,200. Net fuel costs are therefore **£12,300**.

### Working 7

Other running costs are £4,000 per annum x 4 years = **£16,000**.

### Working 8

Tax rebates would be 1,000 miles x 15p (45p-30p) x 4 years x 50% tax = **£300**.

This is how it works out for Rupert:

## Cost of Company Car

| | | |
|---|---|---|
| Tax on benefit | *Working 1* | +£21,200 |
| Net fuel costs | *Working 2* | +£12,460 |
| Private use contributions | *Working 3* | +£2,400 |
| Total costs | | +£36,060 |

## Cost of Own Car

| | | |
|---|---|---|
| Purchase cost less sale proceeds | *Working 4* | +£22,000 |
| Interest on loan | *Working 5* | +£3,800 |
| Net fuel costs | *Working 6* | +£12,300 |
| Other running costs | *Working 7* | +£16,000 |
| Less: Tax rebates on business mileage | *Working 8* | -£300 |
| Total costs | | +£53,800 |

| | |
|---|---|
| **Additional cost of own car over 4 years** | **+£17,740** |
| **Additional cost per annum** | **+£4,435** |

As Rupert pays income tax and national insurance at 52%, he must gross up this figure by 48% to find the equivalent gross pay. He would need a cash alternative of £9,240 per annum in order to be in the same financial position. His employer would deduct tax at 50% and national insurance at 2% giving him net pay of £4,435.

Can his employer afford this? As before, we must work out their savings net of tax and convert to an equivalent salary figure:

### Working 9

Let's assume they can buy the car for £29,000 and sell it after 4 years for £8,000. Their net cost will therefore be £21,000. The capital allowance would have been worth 8% per annum on the written-down value (apart from the first year when it was still worth 10%). After 4 years they would have claimed back only 38.27% of the net cost which is £8,037. The tax saving at 23-26% would have been £1,996, so overall their net saving after tax on the net purchase cost after 4 years would be **£19,004**.

### Working 10

The employer will also save Class 1A national insurance at 13.8% on the benefit. We have already calculated this as £42,400 over the 4 years so 13.8% = £5,851. Deduct corporation tax at an average rate of 24.5% and the total saving is **£4,418**.

### Working 11

They will pay Rupert £1,200 for business mileage at 30p per mile (Working 6). On a company car they would have paid £1,040 (Working 2) which is £160 less. Deduct tax at an average rate of 24.5% and the additional cost is **£121**.

### Working 12

They will also forego the private use contributions of £2,400 which are **£1,812** after deducting tax at 24.5%.

### Working 13

We will assume they save running costs of £5,000 per annum. This is £1,000 a year more than Rupert would pay and assumes they use a main dealer for servicing and incur administration overheads too. Over 4 years they would save £20,000 which is **£15,100** after deducting tax at 24.5%.

### Working 14

We should also factor in their cost of capital. To compare like with like, we'll assume this only arises on the net purchase cost as with Rupert. As before we'll assume they can achieve 5% per annum on the net cash flow of £21,000 (as the sale proceeds on old cars are reinvested each year). That will give them extra income of £1,050 per annum or £4,200 over 4 years. Deduct 24.5% tax and the net amount is **£3,171**.

The overall saving for the employer will be as follows:

| | | |
|---|---|---:|
| Net cost of car | *Working 9* | +£19,004 |
| Employer NI | *Working 10* | +£4,418 |
| Fuel/mileage costs | *Working 11* | -£121 |
| Private use contributions foregone | *Working 12* | -£1,812 |
| Other running costs | *Working 13* | +£15,100 |
| Cost of capital | *Working 14* | +£3,171 |
| **Total savings over 4 years** | | **+£39,760** |
| **Total saving per annum** | | **+£9,940** |

They can afford to pay Rupert a cash alternative of £11,569 per annum out of this saving. The cost to them after adding 13.8% employer national insurance and deducting 24.5% corporation tax would be £9,940 as above.

The cash alternative would be worth £5,553 to him after tax and national insurance at 52%, making him £1,118 a year better off. Rupert should therefore consider giving up his company car and taking the cash alternative instead.

It should be borne in mind that these figures only include 38% of the capital allowance as that is all that has been earned after 4 years. That is because the $CO_2$ emissions exceed 160 g/km and the employer can only therefore claim capital allowances at 8% per annum from April 2012 onwards. However, the employer will earn another 35% over the next 10 years so they could probably afford to increase the Cash Alternative slightly to reflect this.

## Analysis

When you study these two examples, you will see that the major determinant in each case is the tax on the benefit in kind. The other factors tend to offset each other as they affect both employer and employee, but the tax on the benefit only really affects the employee. The employer makes no equivalent saving on this apart from the Class IA national insurance, which even at 13.8% is still a lot less than the income tax paid by the employee.

Obviously a company car is more expensive for the employee when $CO_2$ levels are high and the tax on it is very steep, but the real reason why it can be advantageous to accept a cash alternative in such cases is that the employer is better able to offer a competitive figure. Let me explain why.

At lower $CO_2$ levels the employee is not taxed so much, meaning that the incremental cost of buying and running a car personally is much higher. Therefore the cash alternative needs to go up as the $CO_2$ level goes down in order to keep pace with the higher incremental cost. However, the employer may not be able to offer a competitive figure for a cash alternative in such cases because their own costs are less affected by $CO_2$ levels. Eventually there will come a point where a cash alternative is uneconomic for both the employer and the employee.

Given that the list price of a car is usually only slightly higher than its market value when new and thus affects the employer and the employee to a similar degree, the most important variable in the calculation of the taxable benefit is the $CO_2$ level.

We saw in the first example that, when the taxable benefit was 16% of list price, the employee would have been worse off with a cash alternative by £589 a year. In the second example, when the taxable benefit was the maximum 35%, we saw that the employee would have been better off with a cash alternative by £1,118 a year.

This might lead us to conclude that the breakeven point in this decision is when the Taxable Percentage is about a third of the way between 16% and 35%, say around 23%. The next example should indicate whether or not that is indeed true.


## Case Study # 8.3 – Average Car

Paul is an account manager for Pesky Pizza Leaflets Ltd and drives a company car with a list price of £20,000 and $CO_2$ emissions of 160 g/km. It has a 1600cc engine and runs on diesel. Paul drives 15,000 miles a year of which 7,500 are for business. He pays for all fuel himself and claims business mileage from his employer at an advisory fuel rate of 12p per mile. He is required to pay contributions of £50 per month towards private use of the car.

Paul wonders if he would be better off owning the car himself and taking a cash alternative instead. If he bought the car himself, it would cost him £19,000 and he would have to take out a loan for

4 years at an average rate of 5%. At the end of the 4 years he would sell the car for £4,000 and pay off the balance of the loan. He pays £1.42 per litre for fuel and his fuel consumption is 6 miles per litre. His employer reimburses business mileage for staff using their own cars at 25p per mile. His other running costs would be £3,000 per annum.

Paul earns a salary of £40,000 a year and has taxable investment income of £3,000. His personal allowance is £7,475 and the higher-rate tax band starts at £35,000 (on taxable income). He makes no pension contributions or gift aid donations and there is nothing else that would affect his tax. Basic-rate tax is 20% and higher-rate tax is 40%. How much better off is Paul with a company car?

### *Solution*

### *Working 1*

The $CO_2$ level of 160 g/km falls into the 22% band in 2011/12 and 23% in 2012/13. As the car is a diesel we must add 3% to find the appropriate taxable percentage.

We must also deduct £600 per annum for his private use contributions.

The taxable benefit is therefore £20,000 x 25% - £600 = £4,400 in Year 1 and £20,000 x 26% - £600 = £4,600 in Years 2-4.

Higher-rate tax kicks in at £42,475 and Paul earns £40,000. This means that £2,475 of his car benefit is taxed at 20% and the balance at 40%.

Assuming that tax rates and thresholds remain unchanged (or that his salary keeps pace with any new thresholds) the total tax on his car benefit over the 4 year period works out at **£5,300**.

### *Working 2*

If Paul did not have a company car, almost all his investment income would fall under the higher-rate threshold and he would have only a small amount of extra tax to pay on it. Only £525 would fall into the higher-rate tax bracket which would cost him extra income tax of £105 per annum (as 20% is already deducted at source) which is £420 over 4 years.

As it is, all his investment income falls into the higher-rate tax bracket so he pays additional tax of £600 per annum, which is £2,400 over 4 years. He therefore pays extra tax on his investment income of **£1,980** over the 4 years as a direct result of having a company car.

### Working 3

Total fuel costs are 15,000 miles x £1.42/6 miles per litre x 4 years = £14,200. The employer reimburses 7,500 miles x 12p x 4 years = £3,600. Paul's net fuel costs over the 4 years are therefore **£10,600**.

### Working 4

Private use contributions are £50 x 12 months x 4 years = **£2,400**.

### Working 5

The net cost if Paul bought the car himself would be £19,500 less £4,000 sales proceeds = **£15,500**.

### Working 6

The average balance on his loan would be (£19,500 + £4,000) x 50% = £11,750. Interest at 5% per annum over 4 years would be **£2,350.**

### Working 7

Total fuel costs are £14,200 as per Working 3. The employer will reimburse 7,500 miles x 25p x 4 years = £7,500. Net fuel costs are therefore **£6,700**.

## Working 8

Other running costs are £3,000 per annum x 4 years = **£12,000**.

## Working 9

Tax rebates would be based on 7,500 miles x 15p (40p-25p) = £1,125 per annum. Without a company car he is only £525 over the higher-rate threshold, so £525 of his mileage claim would be allowed at 40% and £600 at 20%.

This would give him a tax rebate of £330 per annum which is **£1,320** over the 4 years.

Putting all these figures together, this is how it works out for Paul:

**Cost of Company Car**

| | | |
|---|---|---|
| Tax on benefit | *Working 1* | +£5,300 |
| Extra tax on investment income | *Working 2* | +£1,980 |
| Net fuel costs | *Working 3* | +£10,600 |
| Private use contributions | *Working 4* | +£2,400 |
| Total costs | | +£20,280 |

**Cost of Own Car**

| | | |
|---|---|---|
| Purchase cost less sale proceeds | *Working 5* | +£15,500 |
| Interest on loan | *Working 6* | +£2,350 |
| Net fuel costs | *Working 7* | +£6,700 |
| Other running costs | *Working 8* | +£12,000 |
| Less: Tax rebates on business mileage | *Working 9* | -£1,320 |
| Total costs | | +£35,230 |

| | |
|---|---|
| **Additional cost of own car over 4 years** | **+£14,950** |
| **Additional cost per annum** | **+£3,738** |

How much would Paul need as a cash equivalent to finance the additional cost? The answer is complicated by the fact that the extra pay would straddle not just the 2 tax bands but also the monthly Class 1 national insurance upper earnings limit (the UEL). Therefore, you cannot just gross up.

Dealing with tax first, the first £2,475 of the cash alternative would be taxed at 20% and the balance at 40%. It also shunts the whole of his investment income into the higher-rate tax bracket, but that would have happened with a company car anyway, so it is irrelevant to the decision.

I'll spare you the number crunching. The gross figure Paul would need as a cash alternative is £6,018. That will give him net pay of £3,738. But can his employer afford this much?

Let's assume that Pesky Pizza Leaflets operates on very tight profit margins and only pays corporation tax at 20%. It does not enjoy fleet discounts so will pay exactly the same for the car as Paul and receive the same sale proceeds on disposal after 4 years. It will pay 20% more in running costs than Paul, which is £3,600 per annum, but can recover VAT on half of this at 20%, which is £300 per annum. The capital allowance will be 66% earned after 4 years giving tax relief at 20% of £1,980. Their cost of capital is 5%. How much would they save if they did not give Paul a company car?

### Working 10

The net cost saved will be the £19,000 purchase price less sale proceeds of £4,000 less tax relief of £1,980 which is **£13,020**.

### Working 11

The taxable benefit is £4,400 in Year 1 and £4,600 in Years 2-4 (Working 1) which comes to £18,200. Employer national insurance is 13.8% which is £2,512. Deduct corporation tax at 20% (national insurance is tax deductible for the company) and the net saving to the employer is **£2,009**.

### Working 12

They will forego private use contributions of £2,400 (Working 4) which after deducting 20% tax is **£1,920**.

## Working 13

Business mileage reimbursed to Paul is £7,500 (Working 7). They would have reimbursed £3,600 on a company car (Working 3). They will therefore pay £3,900 more over the 4 years. Deduct tax at 20% and the net additional cost of mileage is **£3,120**.

## Working 14

They will save other running costs at £3,600 per annum less VAT recoveries of £300 x 4 years = £13,200. Deduct tax at 20% and the net saving is **£10,560**.

## Working 15

Cost of capital after re-investing the sale proceeds would have been £15,000 x 5% x 4 years = £3,000. Deduct tax at 20% and the net saving is **£2,400**.

Therefore, the overall saving to Pesky Pizza Leaflets is as follows:

| | | |
|---|---|---:|
| Net cost of car | *Working 10* | +£13,020 |
| Employer NI | *Working 11* | +£2,010 |
| Private use contributions foregone | *Working 12* | -£1,920 |
| Additional cost of business mileage | *Working 13* | -£3,120 |
| Other running costs | *Working 14* | +£10,560 |
| Cost of capital | *Working 15* | +£2,400 |
| **Total savings over 4 years** | | **+£22,950** |
| **Total saving per annum** | | **+£5,738** |

If we gross this figure up by 80% for tax and deduct employer national insurance at 13.8%, the maximum they can afford to pay Paul as a cash alternative is £6,302.

After deducting tax and national insurance at the various rates applicable, Paul would get net pay of £3,902. Therefore, he would be slightly better of with a cash alternative by £165 per annum.

As with the 2 previous case studies, you should note that these figures only reflect the capital allowances earned after 4 years, in this case 66%. After 10 years the employer will have earned 90%.

Therefore, they could afford to increase the Cash alternative slightly, say by about £200 a year.

It seems that we are almost at the breakeven point for this type of decision. It appears to come at around the 150-154 g/km level for diesel cars and 165-169 g/km for petrol-fuelled cars, where the taxable percentage will be 24% in 2012/13.

In other words, if your company car has $CO_2$ emissions higher than 150 g/km for diesel or 165 g/km for petrol, it would **at first** appear (judging from this example) that you are better off accepting a Cash Alternative instead.

In fact, you might think that this proves the conclusion we began to reach after Case Study # 8.2. However, the next table will demonstrate that the issue is not quite as simple as that.

# Sensitivity Analysis

We are now going to do some sensitivity analysis to see how the results in these three case studies are affected by different $CO_2$ levels. These figures use the 2012/13 rates for the next 2 years too. The table below is based on an average percentage for car benefit over the 4 year period 2011/12 to 2014/15.

| Taxable % | 16% | 18% | 20% | 22% | 24% | 26% | 28% | 30% | 32% | 35% |
|---|---|---|---|---|---|---|---|---|---|---|
| | £ | £ | £ | £ | £ | £ | £ | £ | £ | £ |
| **Max** | | | | | | | | | | |
| Additional cost pa of owning car | 4,366 | 4,306 | 4,246 | 4,186 | 4,126 | 4,066 | 4,006 | 3,946 | 3,886 | 3,796 |
| Maximum Cash Alternative** | 3,777 | 3,802 | 3,827 | 3,851 | 3,876 | 3,901 | 3,925 | 3,950 | 3,975 | 4,012 |
| Shortfall/excess | +589 | +504 | +419 | +335 | +250 | +165 | +81 | -4 | -89 | -216 |
| | | | | | | | | | | |
| **Rupert** | | | | | | | | | | |
| Additional cost pa owning car | 7,475 | 7,155 | 6,835 | 6,515 | 6,195 | 5,875 | 5,555 | 5,235 | 4,915 | 4,435 |
| Maximum Cash Alternative** | 5,199 | 5,236 | 5,274 | 5,311 | 5,348 | 5,385 | 5,423 | 5,460 | 5,497 | 5,553 |
| Shortfall/excess | +2,276 | +1,919 | +1,561 | +1,204 | +847 | +490 | +132 | -225 | -582 | -1,118 |
| | | | | | | | | | | |
| **Paul** | | | | | | | | | | |
| Additional cost pa of owning car | 4,518 | 4,358 | 4,198 | 4,038 | 3,878 | 3,718 | 3,558 | 3,398 | 3,238 | 2,998 |
| Maximum Cash Alternative** | 3,765 | 3,793 | 3,821 | 3,849 | 3,877 | 3,905 | 3,933 | 3,962 | 3,990 | 4,032 |
| Shortfall/excess | +753 | +565 | +377 | +189 | +1 | -187 | -375 | -564 | -752 | -1034 |

** (net of tax & national insurance)

**Additional cost per annum of owning car.** This is the cost of buying and running a car personally that is over and above the cost of having a company car.

**Maximum Cash Alternative.** This is the maximum amount that the employer can afford to pay based on the money they save by not running a company car.

**Shortfall/excess.** This is the difference between the 2 figures. If the number is positive (i.e. a shortfall) it is not viable for the employee to accept a Cash Alternative

### Table 1 Analysis

What do these results tell us?

Firstly, the additional cost of owning your own car gradually decreases at higher $CO_2$ levels. On its own, this makes a Cash Alternative more viable for the employee.

Secondly, the maximum Cash Alternative goes up at higher $CO_2$ levels, which on its own makes a Cash Alternative less viable. However, it goes up at a much slower rate, as the only cost saving for the employer is the Class 1A national insurance.

Both these factors combine to make a Cash Alternative more viable for the employee at higher $CO_2$ levels. In the case of Paul, the viability increases at £188 for every 2% rise.

It should be noted that the effect of higher or lower $CO_2$ levels on capital allowances is not reflected in this table. As we know, cars above 160 g/km only earn capital allowances at 8% per annum from April 2012 compared to 18% per annum for cars with $CO_2$ emissions between 111-160 g/km. However, the effect is fairly negligible and does not alter the overall conclusion.

We can see that at the lowest taxable percentages, a Cash Alternative is not viable for any of them, as there is always a shortfall. For Paul it becomes viable at 24%, which for a diesel car equates to the 150-154 g/km band in 2012/13.

However, for Max and Rupert a different picture emerges. A Cash Alternative does not become viable for them until the Taxable Percentage reaches 29-30%. Clearly something else is affecting the outcome other than $CO_2$ emissions.

In fact, the biggest factor is whether you are a higher-rate taxpayer or a basic-rate taxpayer. For example, if Max paid tax at higher rates, a Cash Alternative would be viable when the benefit-in-kind taxable percentage is 20% or more. For a diesel car this would equate to the 130-134 g/km band in 2012/13.

Why does being a higher-rate taxpayer make it so much more viable to accept a cash alternative? For the same reason that higher $CO_2$ levels do – tax!

188

Obviously higher-rate taxpayers pay more on their car benefit than basic-rate taxpayers – twice as much in fact. At the same time, the cost of buying and running your own car may actually go down, because any tax relief you get on your business mileage will be allowed at your highest rate.

For your employer, on the other hand, the maximum Cash Alternative that it is economic for them to offer stays exactly the same. After all, it makes no difference to them if you pay tax on your car benefit at 40%. The cost to them of providing you with a company car does not alter as a result. However, the tax and national insurance they would have to deduct on a Cash Alternative under PAYE does increase if you are a higher-rate taxpayer, so the net pay you would receive goes down.

One might suppose that higher-rate tax on a Cash Alternative would cancel out the higher-rate tax saved on a company car. The reason it does not is because basic-rate taxpayers suffer national insurance at 12%. Higher-rate taxpayers only suffer national insurance at 2% on every extra pound earned. Therefore, the combined marginal rate of tax and national insurance is 32% for basic-rate taxpayers and 42% for higher-rate taxpayers.

This means that higher-rate taxpayers pay twice as much as basic-rate taxpayers for company cars but less than a third extra for Cash Alternatives. As a result, a higher-rate taxpayer has a greater incentive to accept a Cash Alternative.

However, the saving an employee may make in running costs can also make a crucial difference. For example, if Max had to pay £3,000 a year in running costs (instead of £2,000) it would not be viable for him to accept a Cash Alternative at any $CO_2$ level, not even as a higher-rate tax payer (unless the taxable percentage was the maximum 35%).

Even if Max paid £2,500 a year in running costs (just £500 less than his employers) a Cash Alternative would not be viable for him unless he was a higher-rate taxpayer **and** the taxable percentage on the car benefit-in-kind was 28% or more.

## Key Factors

So we have now identified three key factors in the decision as to whether to accept a cash alternative:

- $CO_2$ levels
- Marginal rate of income tax
- Savings in non-fuel running costs

You can also achieve savings in fuel costs by driving efficiently, filling up at the cheapest garages and using petrol coupons from the supermarket. It tends not to affect this particular decision though as most company car users pay for their own fuel anyway and claim for business mileage at the advisory fuel rates.

Therefore, with regard to fuel costs, it usually makes no difference who owns the car. The number of business miles you drive **does** affect the decision, however, as there is still a significant disparity between the advisory fuel rates and the tax-free mileage rates.

## VAT on Leased Cars

There is another factor that could make it more difficult for an employer to offer a competitive Cash Alternative to its employees and that is the VAT on monthly lease rentals. VAT registered businesses are allowed to reclaim 50% of the VAT on leased cars and lose this if the employee leases the car instead.

To illustrate the effect this can have, we will re-visit Case Study 8.1 and substitute lease rentals for the net capital cost. Instead of buying a car for £14,000 and selling it 4 years later for £5,000 we assume that Pest-Call Windows Ltd leases it for £225 per month (£37.50 is VAT). This figure incorporates their £1,800 cost of capital as a finance charge and spreads the total capital/interest of £10,800 over 48 months, so the cash flows are the same as before.

As Max would have paid £14,500 for the car, sold it for £5,000 and incurred loan interest of £1,950 his total capital/interest would have been £11,450. Therefore, we will set his lease rentals at £238.54 per month including VAT (which of course he cannot recover).

The costs to Max of either having a company car or leasing the car himself are as follows:

**Cost of Company Car**

| | | |
|---|---|---|
| Tax on benefit | *As before* | +£1,920 |
| Private mileage | *As before* | +£2,400 |
| Total costs | | +£4,320 |

**Cost of Own Car**

| | | |
|---|---|---|
| Lease rentals £238.54 x 48 | *As above* | +£11,450 |
| Total fuel costs | *As before* | +£18,933 |
| Less: Mileage reimbursements | *As before* | -£15,000 |
| Less: Tax rebates on business mileage | *As before* | -£1,600 |
| Other running costs | *As before* | +£8,000 |
| Total costs | | +£21,783 |

| | |
|---|---|
| **Additional cost of own car over 4 years** | **+£17,463** |
| **Additional cost per annum** | **+£4,366** |

Obviously the additional cost of leasing the car himself is exactly the same as in the original Case Study. The only changes we have made are to re-categorise the cash-flows.

Now comes the important bit. How much can his employer afford to offer him as a cash alternative? Pest-Call Windows would save the following costs:

| | | |
|---|---|---|
| Lease rentals (£225 x 48) | *As above* | +£10,800 |
| Tax saved on rentals (£10,800 x 24.5%) | *Average rate* | -£2,646 |
| Employer NI | *As before* | +£1,002 |
| Fuel/mileage costs | *As before* | +£1,157 |
| Other running costs (net of VAT) | *As before* | +£8,305 |
| VAT recovered (£37.50 x 48 x 50%) | *As above* | -£900 |
| **Total savings over 4 years** | | **+£17,718** |
| **Total saving per annum** | | **+£4,430** |

In the original case study Pest-Call Windows would have saved £19,089. Therefore, if the car had been leased instead, they would save £1,371 less. This consists of the VAT recovery of £900 plus additional corporation tax savings of £471 (this is because the lease rentals are allowable in full immediately whilst only 77% of the capital allowances could be claimed by the date of disposal if the car was purchased outright).

The annual saving of £4,430 translates to a Cash Alternative of £5,156 after grossing up for corporation tax at an average 24.5% and deducting 13.8% employer national insurance. As Max is a basic-rate taxpayer he would receive 68% of this as net pay (after deducting tax at 20% and national insurance at 12%). Therefore he would get £3,506. Not enough to cover his additional costs of £4,366. He would be adrift by £860 per annum compared to only £589 in the original case study.

This example has been simplified by assuming that the costs of buying and leasing a car are the same. Obviously this is not true, but it enables us to see how much difference the tax effects make.

It also shows clearly that, although leasing cars is generally cheaper for VAT registered businesses than buying them, by the same token it becomes more difficult to offer employees a competitive Cash Alternative.

However, it should be borne in mind that, just because a car is leased, it does not necessarily follow that the employer can recover 50% of the VAT. Certain financial institutions such as banks and insurance companies, whose products are VAT exempt, can only recover a small proportion of input tax on their overheads. Such companies may not need to consider VAT on lease rentals when deciding how much they can afford to offer their employees as an incentive to give up their company cars.

## Summary

This chapter should enable an employee who is offered a Cash Alternative instead of a company car to decide whether it is economic to accept it or not. Likewise, it should enable an employer to work out how much they can afford to offer in the first place. However, the examples we have just examined should never be taken as a direct substitute for your own situation.

You must always choose the numbers relevant to your own circumstances before doing the calculations shown in this chapter.

Running costs may well be the most important factor. Assuming you can keep the lid on these or your employer pays above average for insurance and garage bills, then a Cash Alternative may well be a viable option for you. However, if it looks like you will pay much the same as your employer would, it will be much more difficult to make a Cash Alternative work.

Your marginal tax rate is probably the next most important factor. A Cash Alternative usually works out much better for higher-rate taxpayers than it does for basic-rate taxpayers. If you are right on the cusp of the higher-rate threshold, then you need to take *all* your taxable income into account as your choice could have consequences for your overall tax bill.

Then come $CO_2$ emissions. As we have seen, a Cash Alternative works out better for you the higher your car's taxable percentage. But a high tax bill on your company car does not necessarily mean that you would be better off with a Cash Alternative, as it could be caused mainly by the list price of the car or any optional accessories it may contain.

For example, you could have a luxury car with lots of bells and whistles but reasonably low $CO_2$ emissions. Your tax bill will be high but taking a Cash Alternative will probably not work out better for you as any saving on the tax front will be cancelled out by the cost of buying and running a luxury car.

As we have seen, other factors such as fleet discounts, market values, resale values, business mileage, private use contributions and cost of capital all play their part. These should all be taken into consideration. Obviously they will vary in importance from one case to the next.

You may also be exposed to higher insurance premiums due to your age, claims history or, importantly, the fact that you may require business use on your policy. As a company car driver, the worst that can happen with a speeding offence or a careless prang is a rollicking from your fleet manager. If you own the car yourself, however, you may escape a tongue lashing from the boss but will pay through the nose when your insurance is due for renewal.

If you are one of those drivers who tends to pick up knocks and scrapes, be especially careful as you could end up a lot worse off running your own car. If you see the fleet manager cracking open a bottle of champagne after you've signed the acceptance form for a Cash Alternative, alarm bells should start ringing!

You should also consider your credit history. If you give up your company car for a Cash Alternative, you may need to borrow the money to buy an equivalent car. So make sure you can get a loan!

Employers should bear in mind that, under health and safety regulations, they are still responsible for providing their employees with a safe working environment, even if it happens to be the employee's own car. They must therefore ensure that it is roadworthy, has a current MOT certificate and is regularly serviced. There may also be implications under the Corporate Manslaughter & Homicide Act 2007 for any deaths caused by employees in their own cars whilst doing their jobs. At the very least, this means checking that employees have valid driving licenses before allowing them to use their cars for work.

In general, employers must maintain appropriate policies and procedures to ensure that their employees do not break the law when they are driving on company business, whoever owns the car. For example, if an employee is prosecuted for using a mobile phone whilst driving, or for not wearing glasses if their eyesight is deficient, the police can request a meeting with a director and ask to see relevant policies, risk assessments and evidence of training. An employer can also be prosecuted for accidents caused by their staff as a result of driving excessive hours, or even if they simply failed to monitor their driving hours. It seems that the so-called 'grey fleet' requires almost as much administration as the traditional company car fleet.

Finally, there is one other factor that has not been mentioned yet but is likely to become increasingly important in the current economic climate – the rate of inflation! Company car tax is based on the list price and this is fixed for the life of the car. Therefore, if inflation takes off and salaries go up at the same rate, your company car could become a much smaller part of your overall tax bill. Not only that, but fuel prices and other running costs will also be going up, perhaps by more than you can comfortably afford. You may well be better off with a company car than you realise!

Chapter 15

# Decision # 8
# Should I Join a Salary Sacrifice Scheme?

## How Salary Sacrifice Schemes Work

Salary sacrifice schemes are usually associated with tax-free benefits such as childcare vouchers or pension contributions, so it may seem strange to use them in conjunction with company cars. After all, company cars (apart from electric cars) are definitely not tax free, so how do you benefit under a salary sacrifice arrangement? Basically, there are five ways it can work for you:

- Lower tax
- Fleet discounts
- No employee national insurance
- VAT on the lease rentals
- VAT on the maintenance contract

We will examine each of these factors in turn.

### *Lower Tax*

This is not guaranteed as it depends on the $CO_2$ emissions of the vehicle and also the difference between the list price and the market value of the car. Generally, however, you should be able to save tax on cars with low $CO_2$ emissions (unless they are very expensive) although you should watch out for the changes to the taxable percentages that are due to come into force in April 2012.

Let's suppose that you sacrifice salary of £3,000 a year for a company car. You are given a car with lease rentals of £250 per month (including VAT) for a 3 year term. We can see that over a year this exactly matches the salary foregone. This is important as we can only compare tax on a like-for-like basis if the benefit is of equivalent value to the amount of salary given up.

The car has an average taxable percentage over the 3 years of 15% (remember the percentages tend to go up every year so the average is going to be higher than the one you start with). We shall also assume the car has a list price of £15,000. Therefore, you would be taxed on a car benefit of £2,250 per annum. This is only 75% of the salary you would have been taxed on.

Now let's assume the car has an average taxable percentage of 20%. Each year you would be taxed on a car benefit of £3,000. As this matches the amount of salary given up, you pay exactly the same amount of tax as you would have done otherwise.

Why should the difference between the list price and market value have any effect on tax savings? It is because car rentals (and hence the salary you must sacrifice) are based on market value when new (less the expected residual value at the end of the lease) whilst tax is based on list price.

### Fleet Discounts

It is a well-known fact that major fleet operators obtain significant volume discounts on their cars, whether buying or leasing. This may be slightly offset by administration costs or by lower resale values than a private seller would get, but in general, if you work for a large organisation, it should be cheaper for your employer to provide you with a car than buying or leasing one yourself.

Apparently the trade discount available to bulk buyers can be as much as 40%. That does seem a bit on the high side but illustrates how much cheaper it is for large corporate players. This discount can be used by your employer to offer you a much lower salary sacrifice than you might expect. Alternatively, you may obtain a more expensive car than you could have afforded yourself.

### No Employee National Insurance

This is something of greater importance to basic-rate taxpayers (generally those earning less than £42,475 in 2011/12) who pay national insurance at 12%. Higher-rate taxpayers pay only 2% above that threshold – for the very good reason that it does not count towards their state pension or contribution-based benefits.

There is no employee national insurance on company cars at all, so straight away most basic-rate taxpayers are 12% better off. If you sacrificed £3,000 a year for a company car, you would save employee national insurance of £360. This could enable your employer to lease a more expensive car than you would have been able to afford yourself out of your post-tax salary.

Employers still have to pay 13.8% Class 1A national insurance on the value of the car benefit, but as we have seen this may well be a lot less than the salary foregone. Consequently, there may well be an employer national insurance saving too, which could be ploughed back into the lease rentals, thus benefiting the employee even more.

### VAT on Lease Rentals

If a business is VAT registered it can recover 50% of the VAT on lease rentals, even if a car has only insignificant business use. This VAT recovery can be used by the employer to pay for higher lease rentals than the employee would have been able to afford out of the salary sacrificed.

Say for example an employee sacrifices salary of £3,600 a year. He would have been able to afford lease rentals of £300 per month (including VAT) out of this money. We will set aside the fact that he would have paid tax and national insurance on that salary first as he will pay tax on the car benefit instead. The VAT element is £50 of which the employer can recover £25. The net cost to the employer would therefore be £275 per month.

This would enable the employer to pay lease rentals of £392.70 (including VAT) per month rather than just £360, as it will recover VAT of £32.73 and thereby have a net cost of only £359.97. This is 9% more than the employee would have paid and should result in him/her getting a better car.

Not all employers can recover 50% VAT on lease rentals though. Banks and insurance companies, for example, cannot recover all their input tax on overheads as some or all of their products are VAT exempt. Businesses using the VAT flat rate scheme will also be unable to recover input tax although this generally only applies to small owner-managed companies with an annual turnover of £150,000 or less.

It should also be noted that VAT recovery is not allowed on cars with absolutely no business use whatsoever, so if you wish to take advantage of this benefit you should ensure you do at least one business trip a year.

### *VAT on Maintenance*

Leased cars often come with a maintenance contract whereby, for a fixed monthly sum, the lessor will take care of servicing, repairs, tyres and maintenance not already covered by the warranty. The monthly fees tend to be a bit on the steep side but guarantee that all work is covered, so there are no unexpected garage bills. The advantage of these contracts for a salary sacrifice scheme is that the VAT is 100% recoverable, even if the car has only insignificant business use. This VAT saving can be ploughed back into higher lease rentals.

Obviously the figures involved here are not so large as with the lease rentals and you should also take account of the fact that the maintenance contract will generally cost more than servicing the car at your local friendly (and perfectly well qualified) mechanic.

As with the lease rentals, a VAT recovery is only allowed if a car has at least some business use, so always make sure you do at least one business trip a year.

## Case Study # 9.1

To illustrate all of the above principles, the following case study will show how much money can be saved by a typical employee.

Jenny works as an account manager for Big Fleet Ltd and earns £30,000 a year. Her tax code is 747L and her monthly take-home pay is £1,896.93. She wants a three-year contract on a Ford Ka 1.3Tdci Titanium and has been quoted £178.70 per month (plus VAT) for the lease rental and £21.62 per month (plus VAT) for the maintenance contract. She asks her employer to quote for this car under its salary sacrifice scheme.

Big Fleet Ltd can get a 10% trade discount on the above figures, so its costs are £160.83 per month (plus VAT) for the lease rental and £19.46 per month (plus VAT) for the maintenance contract.

The company can recover 50% of the VAT on the lease rentals and 100% on the maintenance contract. VAT is 20% so the total monthly cost is £160.83 x 1.1 + £19.46 = £196.37.

The car has a list price of £11,251 and is a diesel with $CO_2$ emissions of 109 g/km. The taxable percentage is therefore 13% in 2011/12, 15% in 2012/13 and 16% in 2013/14. Consequently, Jenny's taxable car benefit over the lease term will be as follows:

Year 1 - £1,462
Year 2 - £1,687
Year 3 - £1,800

As employer's national insurance is 13.8%, this would cost Big Fleet Ltd £682.96 over the 3 years.

Let's say the company charges Jenny its net cost of £196.37 per month (see above) by salary sacrifice. Because her salary would be lower, this would save the company employer's national insurance of £27.10 x 36 months = £975.60. Hence the company would save £292.64 over the 3 years which works out at £8.13 per month.

The company could rebate most of this to Jenny and reduce the amount of salary she has to sacrifice to £190 per month. We will assume the salary sacrifice is effective from 6th April 2011 to avoid having to adjust the car benefit in Year 1.

Jenny now earns £2,310 per month instead of £2,500 and her monthly tax and national insurance deductions in each year are as follows:

| Gross Pay | Tax Code | Tax | NI | Net Pay | Annual |
|---|---|---|---|---|---|
| £2,310.00 | 601L | £361.68 | £204.92 | £1,743.40 | £20,920.78 |
| £2,310.00 | 579L | £365.35 | £204.92 | £1,739.73 | £20,876.78 |
| £2,310.00 | 567L | £367.35 | £204.92 | £1,737.73 | £20,852.78 |
| | | | | | £62,650.34 |

These figures assume that Jenny earns the same amount over the three years and that there are no changes in the personal allowance (£7,475), the basic rate of tax (20%) or the national insurance primary threshold (£139 per week).

The reason why her tax code changes is because her car benefit goes up each year.

On this basis, we can see that she would take home £62,650 over the 3 years of the lease.

Had Jenny not entered into the salary sacrifice arrangement and leased the car herself, she would have taken home £68,289 (£1,896.93 x 36) but paid £8,654 for the car (£178.70 x 1.20 x 36 + £21.62 x 1.20 x 36), leaving her with £59,635.

Overall, therefore, she is £3,015 better off with the salary sacrifice over the 3 years, which averages out at £1,005 per annum. This is equivalent to a 4.9% pay rise after grossing up by 68% for tax and national insurance, so it is a very good result. Not many people are getting pay rises like that these days.

## Other Points to Consider

Salary sacrifice schemes generally work out well for employees but there are a few factors you should take into account before going ahead with one.

### *Pensions*

If you are lucky enough to still be in a final salary pension scheme, you should think twice about salary sacrifice if you are approaching retirement age or expect to retire early due to ill health as it could reduce your retirement benefits. You should also ensure that your salary is not reduced so much that you cannot make large one-off contributions to your own personal pension plan, if you were thinking of doing this.

### *Benefits*

Reducing your income with a salary sacrifice may reduce your entitlement to legal payments such as statutory maternity pay, although this is only linked to income for the first six weeks. Similarly, there could be an impact on social security benefits such as income-related Employment Support Allowance, although most benefits these days are means-tested.

### Tax Credits

A lower salary normally means that your entitlement to tax credits goes up although you should ensure that you do not breach the rules on income deprivation. However, a company car benefit is considered earnings for the purposes of calculating working tax credit, and if it is actually higher than the amount of salary sacrificed it could reduce your entitlement.

### Minimum Wage

Under no circumstances should a salary sacrifice scheme reduce earnings below the National Minimum Wage. Benefits-in-kind do not count towards minimum wage.

### Employment Contracts

The salary sacrifice will only work if your employment contract has been properly varied. If you remain legally entitled to the same salary as before, you will still be taxed on the old amount even if you happen to be paid less.

### Disposable Income

It goes without saying that you should never reduce your disposable income to a level insufficient to maintain your standard of living unless you have savings you can fall back on. It is no use reducing your tax bill if you don't have enough money to live on.

### Child Benefit

As most higher-rate taxpayers are now painfully aware, child benefit is to be withdrawn from January 2013 from households where at least one person is paying tax at 40%. Salary sacrifice is often cited as a good way of avoiding that if your income is right on the cusp of the higher-rate bracket. However, in the case of cars you need to be very careful, as the car benefit may not be much less than the salary sacrificed and may even be more. If you are worried about losing your child benefit you may be better off using a salary sacrifice scheme in conjunction with a tax-free benefit, such as pensions or childcare.

# Chapter 16

# Decision # 9
# Is it Worth Having a Fuel Card?

## The Fuel Benefit

As a company car driver, the next big decision for you will be whether to pay for your own fuel or allow your employer to pay for all the fuel you put in the car, perhaps as an alternative to a fuel allowance. On the face of it, this sounds like a no-brainer. Why should you *not* want your employer to pay for all fuel?

The answer of course is that you will be taxed on a fuel benefit. The fuel benefit has now gone up to £18,800 and the taxable percentages have also increased. From April 2012, a petrol-fuelled car with $CO_2$ emissions of 160 g/km falls into the 23% band. A basic-rate taxpayer would therefore pay £865 a year in tax on the fuel benefit:

$$£18,800 \times 23\% \times 20\% \text{ tax} = £865$$

For employers, it has become increasingly expensive to offer this benefit to their staff. Not only do they incur the cost of the fuel, but they also pay Class 1A national insurance at 13.8%.

## Relevant Factors

We can summarise the relevant factors in deciding whether a fuel benefit is worth it or not as follows:

- Your top rate of tax
- The current level of fuel benefit (currently £18,800)
- Your taxable % (based on fuel type and $CO_2$ emissions)
- Your private mileage (including home to work)
- The current price of fuel (and where you buy it)
- Whether fuel prices are stable or going up/down
- The fuel efficiency of your car (miles per gallon/litre)
- How well your car is maintained (eg tyre pressures)

- The way you drive your car (some people use more fuel)
- Where you drive (you use up more fuel in urban areas)
- The type of fuel you use (the taxable benefit is the same for both petrol and diesel)
- The current advisory fuel rates for business mileage
- How much your employer pays for business mileage
- Whether you commute to a temporary workplace or not

## Temporary Workplaces

That last one warrants a bit more explanation. As most people know, travel to/from work does not count as business mileage. You have to treat it as part of your private mileage instead. But that is only true if it is *ordinary* commuting. Travel to/from a temporary workplace is not ordinary commuting and is therefore not private.

That means you can claim expenses from your employer for it (up to the advisory fuel rates for company cars) on a tax-free basis. Or if you pay for all fuel on a corporate card, you do not have to reimburse them for this mileage to avoid a fuel benefit-in-kind (although they may well insist that you reimburse them anyway).

What is a temporary workplace? Well according to HMRC Booklet 480 it is a place where an employee goes only to perform a task of *limited duration* or for a *temporary purpose*.

There are two important points to remember here. First there is the two-year rule. If an employee does not **expect** to be working somewhere for more than two years, then it shall be regarded as a temporary workplace provided he/she was there for a task of limited duration or for a temporary purpose. It is the expectation that counts here. Once an employee *expects* to be working somewhere more than two years, then it is no longer a temporary workplace even if he/she has not been there for two years yet.

Secondly, even if an employee does expect to be working somewhere for more than two years, it can still be treated as a temporary workplace provided that he/she does not carry out their duties to a *significant extent* there. For this purpose, HMRC will regard anyone who spends more than 40% of their working time at one location as ceasing to be at a temporary workplace once the two years have elapsed.

# Fuel Benefit – Common Pitfalls

It can be very easy to trigger a taxable fuel benefit inadvertently even if the intention was for the employee to pay for all private fuel. Remember, if an employer pays just £1 for private fuel, the employee can be landed with a tax bill on a fuel benefit for the whole year. It is therefore extremely important to make sure you don't make any silly mistakes.

The most common mistake is to claim business mileage for journeys that were substantially ordinary commuting. If an employee stops on the way home from work to visit a customer or supplier, that is not a business trip. It is the main purpose of the journey that counts. Incidental errands outside working hours do not count unless they require a significant detour. Getting the mileage wrong or claiming more than the advisory fuel rates for business trips is another common error.

Where an employer pays for all fuel up front, say on a corporate card, and requires the employee to reimburse private mileage, it is very important that the employee does actually reimburse the private mileage by the end of the tax year, or very soon afterwards. It is often better for the employee to pay for all fuel up front and then claim business mileage from the employer.

Do not mix up private mileage payments with private use contributions or reimbursements of other kinds, such as towards other running costs. It is important to keep sufficient back-up for both reimbursements and expense claims, so there is no argument about what they were for or how they were calculated. This should include a mileage log and details such as dates, locations and reasons for business travel. The advisory fuel rates are updated fairly regularly so you need to know when mileage was incurred so you can apply the correct rates.

If you work through your own limited company, it is generally not a good idea to pay for all fuel through the company. You will not be saving anything on the fuel as it is effectively your money anyway, plus you will incur both tax and Class 1A on a fuel benefit. However, you can still claim corporation tax relief on business mileage and VAT at the advisory fuel rates, so you will not lose out in that respect.

# Breakeven Mileage

The following tables illustrate the tax efficiency of private fuel paid for by your employer at various mileage levels right up to an apocalyptic £2 per litre.

## Example 1

The table below assumes that the driver is a basic-rate taxpayer, the car does 6.6 miles to the litre and the taxable charge on the fuel benefit is 23%. His income tax liability on the fuel is £865:

£18,800 x 23% benefit-in-kind charge x 20% income tax

## Fuel Costs Less Tax on Benefit – Basic-rate Taxpayer

| Petrol | Private Mileage | | | | | | | | | |
|--------|--------|--------|--------|--------|--------|--------|--------|--------|--------|--------|
|  | 3,000 | 4,000 | 5,000 | 6,000 | 7,000 | 8,000 | 9,000 | 10,000 | 11,000 | 12,000 |
| £1.00 | -£410 | -£259 | -£107 | £44 | £196 | £347 | £499 | £650 | £802 | £953 |
| £1.05 | -£388 | -£228 | -£69 | £90 | £249 | £408 | £567 | £726 | £885 | £1,044 |
| £1.10 | -£365 | -£198 | -£31 | £135 | £302 | £469 | £635 | £802 | £969 | £1,135 |
| £1.15 | -£342 | -£168 | £6 | £181 | £355 | £529 | £703 | £878 | £1,052 | £1,226 |
| £1.20 | -£319 | -£138 | £44 | £226 | £408 | £590 | £772 | £953 | £1,135 | £1,317 |
| £1.25 | -£297 | -£107 | £82 | £272 | £461 | £650 | £840 | £1,029 | £1,219 | £1,408 |
| £1.30 | -£274 | -£77 | £120 | £317 | £514 | £711 | £908 | £1,105 | £1,302 | £1,499 |
| £1.35 | -£251 | -£47 | £158 | £362 | £567 | £772 | £976 | £1,181 | £1,385 | £1,590 |
| £1.40 | -£228 | -£16 | £196 | £408 | £620 | £832 | £1,044 | £1,256 | £1,469 | £1,681 |
| £1.45 | -£206 | £14 | £234 | £453 | £673 | £893 | £1,112 | £1,332 | £1,552 | £1,772 |
| £1.50 | -£183 | £44 | £272 | £499 | £726 | £953 | £1,181 | £1,408 | £1,635 | £1,862 |
| £1.55 | -£160 | £75 | £309 | £544 | £779 | £1,014 | £1,249 | £1,484 | £1,719 | £1,953 |
| £1.60 | -£138 | £105 | £347 | £590 | £832 | £1,075 | £1,317 | £1,559 | £1,802 | £2,044 |
| £1.65 | -£115 | £135 | £385 | £635 | £885 | £1,135 | £1,385 | £1,635 | £1,885 | £2,135 |
| £1.70 | -£92 | £166 | £423 | £681 | £938 | £1,196 | £1,453 | £1,711 | £1,969 | £2,226 |
| £1.75 | -£69 | £196 | £461 | £726 | £991 | £1,256 | £1,522 | £1,787 | £2,052 | £2,317 |
| £1.80 | -£47 | £226 | £499 | £772 | £1,044 | £1,317 | £1,590 | £1,862 | £2,135 | £2,408 |
| £1.85 | -£24 | £256 | £537 | £817 | £1,097 | £1,378 | £1,658 | £1,938 | £2,219 | £2,499 |
| £1.90 | -£1 | £287 | £575 | £862 | £1,150 | £1,438 | £1,726 | £2,014 | £2,302 | £2,590 |
| £1.95 | £22 | £317 | £612 | £908 | £1,203 | £1,499 | £1,794 | £2,090 | £2,385 | £2,681 |
| £2.00 | £44 | £347 | £650 | £953 | £1,256 | £1,559 | £1,862 | £2,166 | £2,469 | £2,772 |

The table shows that if you do 5,000 private miles per year and the price per litre is £1.30 per litre you will be £120 better off if your employer pays for private fuel.

## Example 2

Now let's consider a higher-rate taxpayer driving a diesel car that does 8.5 miles to the litre and has a taxable charge on the fuel benefit of 30%. His income tax liability on the fuel will be £2,256.

### Fuel Costs Less Tax on Benefit – Higher-rate Taxpayer

| Diesel | | | | | | | | | | |
|---|---|---|---|---|---|---|---|---|---|---|

| Diesel | 3,000 | 4,000 | 5,000 | 6,000 | 7,000 | 8,000 | 9,000 | 10,0000 | 11,000 | 12,000 |
|---|---|---|---|---|---|---|---|---|---|---|
| £1.00 | -£1,903 | -£1,785 | -£1,668 | -£1,550 | -£1,432 | -£1,315 | -£1,197 | -£1,080 | -£962 | -£844 |
| £1.05 | -£1,885 | -£1,762 | -£1,638 | -£1,515 | -£1,391 | -£1,268 | -£1,144 | -£1,021 | -£897 | -£774 |
| £1.10 | -£1,868 | -£1,738 | -£1,609 | -£1,480 | -£1,350 | -£1,221 | -£1,091 | -£962 | -£832 | -£703 |
| £1.15 | -£1,850 | -£1,715 | -£1,580 | -£1,444 | -£1,309 | -£1,174 | -£1,038 | -£903 | -£768 | -£632 |
| £1.20 | -£1,832 | -£1,691 | -£1,550 | -£1,409 | -£1,268 | -£1,127 | -£985 | -£844 | -£703 | -£562 |
| £1.25 | -£1,815 | -£1,668 | -£1,521 | -£1,374 | -£1,227 | -£1,080 | -£932 | -£785 | -£638 | -£491 |
| £1.30 | -£1,797 | -£1,644 | -£1,491 | -£1,338 | -£1,185 | -£1,032 | -£880 | -£727 | -£574 | -£421 |
| £1.35 | -£1,780 | -£1,621 | -£1,462 | -£1,303 | -£1,144 | -£985 | -£827 | -£668 | -£509 | -£350 |
| £1.40 | -£1,762 | -£1,597 | -£1,432 | -£1,268 | -£1,103 | -£938 | -£774 | -£609 | -£444 | -£280 |
| £1.45 | -£1,744 | -£1,574 | -£1,403 | -£1,232 | -£1,062 | -£891 | -£721 | -£550 | -£380 | -£209 |
| £1.50 | -£1,727 | -£1,550 | -£1,374 | -£1,197 | -£1,021 | -£844 | -£668 | -£491 | -£315 | -£138 |
| £1.55 | -£1,709 | -£1,527 | -£1,344 | -£1,162 | -£980 | -£797 | -£615 | -£432 | -£250 | -£68 |
| £1.60 | -£1,691 | -£1,503 | -£1,315 | -£1,127 | -£938 | -£750 | -£562 | -£374 | -£185 | £3 |
| £1.65 | -£1,674 | -£1,480 | -£1,285 | -£1,091 | -£897 | -£703 | -£509 | -£315 | -£121 | £73 |
| £1.70 | -£1,656 | -£1,456 | -£1,256 | -£1,056 | -£856 | -£656 | -£456 | -£256 | -£56 | £144 |
| £1.75 | -£1,638 | -£1,432 | -£1,227 | -£1,021 | -£815 | -£609 | -£403 | -£197 | £9 | £215 |
| £1.80 | -£1,621 | -£1,409 | -£1,197 | -£985 | -£774 | -£562 | -£350 | -£138 | £73 | £285 |
| £1.85 | -£1,603 | -£1,385 | -£1,168 | -£950 | -£732 | -£515 | -£297 | -£80 | £138 | £356 |
| £1.90 | -£1,585 | -£1,362 | -£1,138 | -£915 | -£691 | -£468 | -£244 | -£21 | £203 | £426 |
| £1.95 | -£1,568 | -£1,338 | -£1,109 | -£880 | -£650 | -£421 | -£191 | £38 | £268 | £497 |
| £2.00 | -£1,550 | -£1,315 | -£1,080 | -£844 | -£609 | -£374 | -£138 | £97 | £332 | £568 |

A quite different picture now emerges. We can see that private fuel paid for by your employer does not become tax efficient until the fuel price reaches £1.60 per litre and mileage is at least 12,000. At 10,000 miles the breakeven price is £1.92 per litre.

## Analysis

Why do these two examples show such different results? The most obvious answer is that higher-rate tax at 40% is double basic-rate tax. Therefore, breakeven mileage must also double. However, in this case we also had a higher taxable percentage on the car – 30% compared with 23%. Then there is the fuel consumption rate. You normally get about 30% more mileage from diesel compared to unleaded petrol (although diesel normally costs about 5% more) which increases the breakeven point still further. Put these three factors together and you get the results shown above.

## Non Company Car Drivers

Sometimes employers offer fuel cards to staff using their own cars. Such employees are not affected by the fixed rate fuel benefit. Instead they are taxed on the exact cost of the fuel paid for by their employer. These people will always be better off with a fuel card, because the tax they pay on it can never be more than 40% of their fuel costs (or 50% if they are additional rate taxpayers). It is important to check your P11D if you use your own car in case the employer taxes you on a company car by mistake. This can easily happen if the employer knows the $CO_2$ emissions for your vehicle but forgets to note that the car actually belongs to you!

One area where non company car drivers with fuel cards often lose out is on business mileage. Anyone who does *not* get free private fuel will already understand the importance of keeping good mileage records and making regular claims, but if your employer gives you a fuel card and does not expect private miles to be reimbursed, it can be easy to overlook the business miles element. For company car drivers it does not matter as you are taxed on the same figure regardless of how many business miles you drive. For people driving their own cars, however, it very much does matter.

In fact, whilst going through a client's records a few years ago I noticed a strange item on his P11D which he said was a fuel card. As he was a higher-rate taxpayer, I pointed out to him that it probably wasn't to his advantage to have private fuel paid for by his employer, to which he said that it was for his own car, not a company car. I can still see his face now when I told him he should have been claiming 40p a mile for all his business journeys from the taxman.

Had he kept a mileage log? Of course not. The notion of claiming a tax rebate for business miles hadn't even occurred to him, as it wouldn't for most people. All he could do was try and estimate how many business miles he'd driven each year based on his usual pattern of work. Fortunately the taxman will accept such estimates provided they are reasonable.

How do you even begin to estimate business mileage going back up to 6 years? Well most people who drive their cars for work tend to have both regular journeys and occasional journeys. You don't have to remember all the occasional ones although the one-off trips will probably stick in your mind, particularly if they were a long way. However, the regular journeys are the ones you really want. Most people can remember where they used to go on a regular basis and how far away it was. Then you just need to multiply by the number of times you went. Here it is best to take an average, such as twice a week or three times a month.

Where you are basing mileage allowances on estimates, it is wise to check them against total mileage so you can prove they are not excessive. Here you have some help as you can go by the P11D figure, which should be the amount you spent on your fuel card.

Then you need to look up historic fuel costs, which you can find on the monthly AA Fuel Reports at:

www.theaa.com/motoring_advice/fuel

They show average fuel prices for each year too so you don't have to look up each individual month, although you would need to take a bit of artistic license and treat calendar years as tax years. This will give you an estimate of litres purchased for each tax year.

The final step is to estimate total mileage by multiplying litres purchased by miles per litre (or miles per gallon divided by 4.546) based on the fuel efficiency of your car. A reasonable estimate will do here. The fuel consumption rates published by the manufacturer for your make/model should suffice. Obviously the higher this figure is the higher your estimate of total mileage will be, and the higher that figure is then the more reasonable your estimate of business mileage will look. However, you should also make sure the balancing figure (for private mileage) looks reasonable, as few people drive less than 5,000 miles a year.

# Private Fuel for Company Vans

People with company vans do not need to worry about the £18,800 fixed rate fuel benefit as they have their own fixed rate, which is £550 from 6th April 2011.

At first sight this may seem incredibly generous (if you can ever call a tax generous) but you have to remember that people tend not to drive that many private miles in their vans. Many van drivers have their own cars for domestic use. For instance, you wouldn't want to turn up for a family wedding in a dirty old van! However, there may be some occasions when a van is useful for domestic use too.

Company van drivers have an advantage here as home-to-work travel is allowed for tax purposes. They are also allowed some domestic use too, so long as it is insignificant, such as taking rubbish to the dump once a year. Anything beyond that, such as taking the kids to school (unless it is on the way to work) or doing the weekly shopping, incurs the flat rate van benefit-in-kind of £3,000 and the van fuel benefit of £550.

So is it worth it? Well let's say you only use the van to do the weekly shopping (a six mile round trip 50 times a year) and a couple of times a year for occasions where you need to transport equipment (such as car boot sales or a windsurfing weekend). If we estimate 100 miles for each special trip, that would give an annual total of 500 miles – not an awful lot. If we assume diesel is £1.45 a litre and the van does 20 miles to the gallon around town (or 4.4 miles to the litre) that would cost £165 a year. A basic-rate taxpayer would pay £110 on the fuel benefit at 20%, so he would be £55 a year better off with private fuel paid for by his employer.

The breakeven point for a basic-rate taxpayer is 334 miles. In other words if you do more than 334 private miles per year your employer should pay for your private fuel. For a higher-rate taxpayer it would be double that. On the whole, therefore, it would seem worthwhile for a company van driver to accept employer paid private fuel, especially with the price of diesel going up all the time. And it would save all the hassle of keeping a mileage log too.

# Chapter 17

# Decision # 10
# Which Type of Company Car
# Should I Have?

## Car Benefit Tables

Company car drivers will have many different reasons for choosing a particular car to drive and tax is just one of many considerations, albeit a very important one.

It is beyond the realm of this book to consider all the other various factors that may sway an employee's choice of car. We must focus on the tax issues, and for a company car driver the main thing he/she will want to know is how much tax they will have to pay.

The table below shows the taxable percentages for the 2011/12 tax year and the taxable benefit-in-kind at various list prices.

Tax payable on these amounts will be 20% for basic-rate taxpayers, 40% for higher-rate taxpayers and 50% for additional rate taxpayers.

Note that if you make a capital contribution of up to £5,000 towards your company car this should be deducted from the list price. If you make personal use contributions you should deduct the annual total from the figures in the table.

You should also add on the list price of accessories not already included as standard fittings in your car.

## 2011/12 Taxable Benefit in Kind (£)

| CO2 g/km | Taxable % | Manufacturer's List Price | | | | | | | | |
|---|---|---|---|---|---|---|---|---|---|---|
| | | 10,000 | 12,000 | 14,000 | 16,000 | 18,000 | 20,000 | 24,000 | 26,000 | 30,000 |
| 76-120 | 10% | 1,000 | 1,200 | 1,400 | 1,600 | 1,800 | 2,000 | 2,400 | 2,600 | 3,000 |
| 121-129 | 15% | 1,500 | 1,800 | 2,100 | 2,400 | 2,700 | 3,000 | 3,600 | 3,900 | 4,500 |
| 130-134 | 16% | 1,600 | 1,920 | 2,240 | 2,560 | 2,880 | 3,200 | 3,840 | 4,160 | 4,800 |
| 135-139 | 17% | 1,700 | 2,040 | 2,380 | 2,720 | 3,060 | 3,400 | 4,080 | 4,420 | 5,100 |
| 140-144 | 18% | 1,800 | 2,160 | 2,520 | 2,880 | 3,240 | 3,600 | 4,320 | 4,680 | 5,400 |
| 145-149 | 19% | 1,900 | 2,280 | 2,660 | 3,040 | 3,420 | 3,800 | 4,560 | 4,940 | 5,700 |
| 150-154 | 20% | 2,000 | 2,400 | 2,800 | 3,200 | 3,600 | 4,000 | 4,800 | 5,200 | 6,000 |
| 155-159 | 21% | 2,100 | 2,520 | 2,940 | 3,360 | 3,780 | 4,200 | 5,040 | 5,460 | 6,300 |
| 160-164 | 22% | 2,200 | 2,640 | 3,080 | 3,520 | 3,960 | 4,400 | 5,280 | 5,720 | 6,600 |
| 165-169 | 23% | 2,300 | 2,760 | 3,220 | 3,680 | 4,140 | 4,600 | 5,520 | 5,980 | 6,900 |
| 170-174 | 24% | 2,400 | 2,880 | 3,360 | 3,840 | 4,320 | 4,800 | 5,760 | 6,240 | 7,200 |
| 175-179 | 25% | 2,500 | 3,000 | 3,500 | 4,000 | 4,500 | 5,000 | 6,000 | 6,500 | 7,500 |
| 180-184 | 26% | 2,600 | 3,120 | 3,640 | 4,160 | 4,680 | 5,200 | 6,240 | 6,760 | 7,800 |
| 185-189 | 27% | 2,700 | 3,240 | 3,780 | 4,320 | 4,860 | 5,400 | 6,480 | 7,020 | 8,100 |
| 190-194 | 28% | 2,800 | 3,360 | 3,920 | 4,480 | 5,040 | 5,600 | 6,720 | 7,280 | 8,400 |
| 195-199 | 29% | 2,900 | 3,480 | 4,060 | 4,640 | 5,220 | 5,800 | 6,960 | 7,540 | 8,700 |
| 200-204 | 30% | 3,000 | 3,600 | 4,200 | 4,800 | 5,400 | 6,000 | 7,200 | 7,800 | 9,000 |
| 204-209 | 31% | 3,100 | 3,720 | 4,340 | 4,960 | 5,580 | 6,200 | 7,440 | 8,060 | 9,300 |
| 210-214 | 32% | 3,200 | 3,840 | 4,480 | 5,120 | 5,760 | 6,400 | 7,680 | 8,320 | 9,600 |
| 215-219 | 33% | 3,300 | 3,960 | 4,620 | 5,280 | 5,940 | 6,600 | 7,920 | 8,580 | 9,900 |
| 220-224 | 34% | 3,400 | 4,080 | 4,760 | 5,440 | 6,120 | 6,800 | 8,160 | 8,840 | 10,200 |
| 225 + | 35% | 3,500 | 4,200 | 4,900 | 5,600 | 6,300 | 7,000 | 8,400 | 9,100 | 10,500 |

## Note:

Diesels are taxed 3% higher than the bands shown above subject to a 35% maximum.

## Tax Thresholds for 2011/12

Personal Allowance - £7,475
Higher-rate Threshold - £35,000
Earnings at Basic-rate - £42,475
Additional Rate Threshold - £150,000

The table below shows the same information for the 2012/13 tax year. You will see that the tax will be going up next year, especially for those driving cars with $CO_2$ emissions between 100-120 g/km.

**2012/13 Taxable Benefit in Kind (£)**

| | | Manufacturer's List Price | | | | | | | | |
|---|---|---|---|---|---|---|---|---|---|---|
| **CO2 g/km** | **Taxable** | **10,000** | **12,000** | **14,000** | **16,000** | **18,000** | **20,000** | **24,000** | **26,000** | **30,000** |
| 76-99 | 10% | 1,000 | 1,200 | 1,400 | 1,600 | 1,800 | 2,000 | 2,400 | 2,600 | 3,000 |
| 100-104 | 11% | 1,100 | 1,320 | 1,540 | 1,760 | 1,980 | 2,200 | 2,640 | 2,860 | 3,300 |
| 105-109 | 12% | 1,200 | 1,440 | 1,680 | 1,920 | 2,160 | 2,400 | 2,880 | 3,120 | 3,600 |
| 110-114 | 13% | 1,300 | 1,560 | 1,820 | 2,080 | 2,340 | 2,600 | 3,120 | 3,380 | 3,900 |
| 115-119 | 14% | 1,400 | 1,680 | 1,960 | 2,240 | 2,520 | 2,800 | 3,360 | 3,640 | 4,200 |
| 120-124 | 15% | 1,500 | 1,800 | 2,100 | 2,400 | 2,700 | 3,000 | 3,600 | 3,900 | 4,500 |
| 125-129 | 16% | 1,600 | 1,920 | 2,240 | 2,560 | 2,880 | 3,200 | 3,840 | 4,160 | 4,800 |
| 130-134 | 17% | 1,700 | 2,040 | 2,380 | 2,720 | 3,060 | 3,400 | 4,080 | 4,420 | 5,100 |
| 135-139 | 18% | 1,800 | 2,160 | 2,520 | 2,880 | 3,240 | 3,600 | 4,320 | 4,680 | 5,400 |
| 140-144 | 19% | 1,900 | 2,280 | 2,660 | 3,040 | 3,420 | 3,800 | 4,560 | 4,940 | 5,700 |
| 145-149 | 20% | 2,000 | 2,400 | 2,800 | 3,200 | 3,600 | 4,000 | 4,800 | 5,200 | 6,000 |
| 150-154 | 21% | 2,100 | 2,520 | 2,940 | 3,360 | 3,780 | 4,200 | 5,040 | 5,460 | 6,300 |
| 155-159 | 22% | 2,200 | 2,640 | 3,080 | 3,520 | 3,960 | 4,400 | 5,280 | 5,720 | 6,600 |
| 160-164 | 23% | 2,300 | 2,760 | 3,220 | 3,680 | 4,140 | 4,600 | 5,520 | 5,980 | 6,900 |
| 165-169 | 24% | 2,400 | 2,880 | 3,360 | 3,840 | 4,320 | 4,800 | 5,760 | 6,240 | 7,200 |
| 170-174 | 25% | 2,500 | 3,000 | 3,500 | 4,000 | 4,500 | 5,000 | 6,000 | 6,500 | 7,500 |
| 175-179 | 26% | 2,600 | 3,120 | 3,640 | 4,160 | 4,680 | 5,200 | 6,240 | 6,760 | 7,800 |
| 180-184 | 27% | 2,700 | 3,240 | 3,780 | 4,320 | 4,860 | 5,400 | 6,480 | 7,020 | 8,100 |
| 185-189 | 28% | 2,800 | 3,360 | 3,920 | 4,480 | 5,040 | 5,600 | 6,720 | 7,280 | 8,400 |
| 190-194 | 29% | 2,900 | 3,480 | 4,060 | 4,640 | 5,220 | 5,800 | 6,960 | 7,540 | 8,700 |
| 195-199 | 30% | 3,000 | 3,600 | 4,200 | 4,800 | 5,400 | 6,000 | 7,200 | 7,800 | 9,000 |
| 200-204 | 31% | 3,100 | 3,720 | 4,340 | 4,960 | 5,580 | 6,200 | 7,440 | 8,060 | 9,300 |
| 204-209 | 32% | 3,200 | 3,840 | 4,480 | 5,120 | 5,760 | 6,400 | 7,680 | 8,320 | 9,600 |
| 210-214 | 33% | 3,300 | 3,960 | 4,620 | 5,280 | 5,940 | 6,600 | 7,920 | 8,580 | 9,900 |
| 215-219 | 34% | 3,400 | 4,080 | 4,760 | 5,440 | 6,120 | 6,800 | 8,160 | 8,840 | 10,200 |
| 220 + | 35% | 3,500 | 4,200 | 4,900 | 5,600 | 6,300 | 7,000 | 8,400 | 9,100 | 10,500 |

**Note:**
Diesels are taxed 3% higher than the bands shown above subject to a 35% maximum.

The tax thresholds and personal allowance for 2012/13 had not been announced at the time of writing.

The table below shows the same information for the 2013/14 tax year. As usual the tax bands are going up by 1%.

## 2013/14 Taxable Benefit in Kind (£)

| CO2 (g/km) | Taxable % | Manufacturer's List Price | | | | | | | | |
|---|---|---|---|---|---|---|---|---|---|---|
| | | 10,000 | 12,000 | 14,000 | 16,000 | 18,000 | 20,000 | 24,000 | 26,000 | 30,000 |
| 76-94 | 10% | 1,000 | 1,200 | 1,400 | 1,600 | 1,800 | 2,000 | 2,400 | 2,600 | 3,000 |
| 95-99 | 11% | 1,100 | 1,320 | 1,540 | 1,760 | 1,980 | 2,200 | 2,640 | 2,860 | 3,300 |
| 100-104 | 12% | 1,200 | 1,440 | 1,680 | 1,920 | 2,160 | 2,400 | 2,880 | 3,120 | 3,600 |
| 105-109 | 13% | 1,300 | 1,560 | 1,820 | 2,080 | 2,340 | 2,600 | 3,120 | 3,380 | 3,900 |
| 110-114 | 14% | 1,400 | 1,680 | 1,960 | 2,240 | 2,520 | 2,800 | 3,360 | 3,640 | 4,200 |
| 115-119 | 15% | 1,500 | 1,800 | 2,100 | 2,400 | 2,700 | 3,000 | 3,600 | 3,900 | 4,500 |
| 120-124 | 16% | 1,600 | 1,920 | 2,240 | 2,560 | 2,880 | 3,200 | 3,840 | 4,160 | 4,800 |
| 125-129 | 17% | 1,700 | 2,040 | 2,380 | 2,720 | 3,060 | 3,400 | 4,080 | 4,420 | 5,100 |
| 130-134 | 18% | 1,800 | 2,160 | 2,520 | 2,880 | 3,240 | 3,600 | 4,320 | 4,680 | 5,400 |
| 135-139 | 19% | 1,900 | 2,280 | 2,660 | 3,040 | 3,420 | 3,800 | 4,560 | 4,940 | 5,700 |
| 140-144 | 20% | 2,000 | 2,400 | 2,800 | 3,200 | 3,600 | 4,000 | 4,800 | 5,200 | 6,000 |
| 145-149 | 21% | 2,100 | 2,520 | 2,940 | 3,360 | 3,780 | 4,200 | 5,040 | 5,460 | 6,300 |
| 150-154 | 22% | 2,200 | 2,640 | 3,080 | 3,520 | 3,960 | 4,400 | 5,280 | 5,720 | 6,600 |
| 155-159 | 23% | 2,300 | 2,760 | 3,220 | 3,680 | 4,140 | 4,600 | 5,520 | 5,980 | 6,900 |
| 160-164 | 24% | 2,400 | 2,880 | 3,360 | 3,840 | 4,320 | 4,800 | 5,760 | 6,240 | 7,200 |
| 165-169 | 25% | 2,500 | 3,000 | 3,500 | 4,000 | 4,500 | 5,000 | 6,000 | 6,500 | 7,500 |
| 170-174 | 26% | 2,600 | 3,120 | 3,640 | 4,160 | 4,680 | 5,200 | 6,240 | 6,760 | 7,800 |
| 175-179 | 27% | 2,700 | 3,240 | 3,780 | 4,320 | 4,860 | 5,400 | 6,480 | 7,020 | 8,100 |
| 180-184 | 28% | 2,800 | 3,360 | 3,920 | 4,480 | 5,040 | 5,600 | 6,720 | 7,280 | 8,400 |
| 185-189 | 29% | 2,900 | 3,480 | 4,060 | 4,640 | 5,220 | 5,800 | 6,960 | 7,540 | 8,700 |
| 190-194 | 30% | 3,000 | 3,600 | 4,200 | 4,800 | 5,400 | 6,000 | 7,200 | 7,800 | 9,000 |
| 195-199 | 31% | 3,100 | 3,720 | 4,340 | 4,960 | 5,580 | 6,200 | 7,440 | 8,060 | 9,300 |
| 200-204 | 32% | 3,200 | 3,840 | 4,480 | 5,120 | 5,760 | 6,400 | 7,680 | 8,320 | 9,600 |
| 204-209 | 33% | 3,300 | 3,960 | 4,620 | 5,280 | 5,940 | 6,600 | 7,920 | 8,580 | 9,900 |
| 210-214 | 34% | 3,400 | 4,080 | 4,760 | 5,440 | 6,120 | 6,800 | 8,160 | 8,840 | 10,200 |
| 215 + | 35% | 3,500 | 4,200 | 4,900 | 5,600 | 6,300 | 7,000 | 8,400 | 9,100 | 10,500 |

## Note

Diesels are taxed 3% higher than the bands shown above subject to a 35% maximum.

The tax thresholds and personal allowance for 2013/14 had not been announced at the time of writing.

# Popular Cars

For company car users looking to reduce their tax bills, the most obvious advice is to choose a car with low $CO_2$ emissions or list price, preferably both. This also helps employers, as it reduces their Class 1A national insurance contributions. The table below shows some of the more popular makes and models and the income tax you would have to pay on each car at both 20% and 40%.

## Taxable Payable on Popular Cars

| Make | Fuel | List Price | CO2 | 11/12 Tax % | 11/12 P11D | 11/12 20% Tax | 12/13 20% Tax | 11/12 40% Tax | 12/13 40% Tax | Up by |
|------|------|-----------|-----|-------------|------------|---------------|---------------|---------------|---------------|-------|
| Audi A3 1.6 TDI | D | £18,835 | 99 | 13% | £2,449 | £490 | £490 | £979 | £979 | 0.0% |
| Audi A6 Avant New | D | £31,930 | 132 | 19% | £6,067 | £1,213 | £1,277 | £2,427 | £2,554 | 5.3% |
| BMW 318d SE Auto | D | £28,150 | 140 | 21% | £5,912 | £1,182 | £1,239 | £2,365 | £2,477 | 4.8% |
| BMW 523i SE Manual | P | £32,345 | 177 | 25% | £8,086 | £1,617 | £1,682 | £3,235 | £3,364 | 4.0% |
| Fiat Punto 1.2 Active | P | £10,740 | 123 | 15% | £1,611 | £322 | £322 | £644 | £644 | 0.0% |
| Ford Fiesta Edge 60PS | P | £10,790 | 127 | 15% | £1,619 | £324 | £345 | £647 | £691 | 6.5% |
| Ford Focus 1.6i Zetec | P | £15,967 | 159 | 21% | £3,353 | £671 | £703 | £1,341 | £1,405 | 4.8% |
| Ford Mondeo 1.6 Zetec | P | £20,640 | 114 | 13% | £2,683 | £537 | £660 | £1,073 | £1,321 | 23.0% |
| Ford Ka 1.2 8V Studio | P | £8,490 | 115 | 10% | £849 | £170 | £238 | £340 | £475 | 40.0% |
| Honda Accord 2.2 ES | D | £24,525 | 170 | 27% | £6,622 | £1,324 | £1,373 | £2,649 | £2,747 | 3.7% |
| Hyundai 1.6 GDI Style | P | £20,195 | 155 | 21% | £4,195 | £839 | £879 | £1,678 | £1,758 | 4.8% |
| Jaguar XF 5.0 V8 | P | £51,895 | 264 | 35% | £18,163 | £3,633 | £3,633 | £7,265 | £7,265 | 0.0% |
| Jeep Wrangler 2.8 | P | £22,995 | 187 | 30% | £6,749 | £1,350 | £1,395 | £2,699 | £2,789 | 3.3% |
| Nissan Micra 1.2 | P | £10,795 | 115 | 10% | £1,080 | £216 | £302 | £432 | £605 | 40.0% |
| Peugeot 308 1.4 VTi | P | £16,110 | 144 | 18% | £2,900 | £580 | £612 | £1,160 | £1,224 | 5.5% |
| Seat Altea 1.6 TDi SE | D | £18,620 | 119 | 13% | £2,421 | £484 | £633 | £968 | £1,266 | 30.8% |
| Renault Megane 1.6 | P | £15,470 | 159 | 21% | £3,249 | £650 | £681 | £1,299 | £1,361 | 4.8% |
| Toyota Verso 2.0 | D | £19,620 | 139 | 20% | £3,924 | £785 | £824 | £1,570 | £1,648 | 5.0% |
| Vauxhall Agila 1.0i | P | £10,380 | 119 | 10% | £1,038 | £208 | £291 | £415 | £581 | 40.0% |
| Vauxhall Astra 1.6i | P | £20,940 | 147 | 19% | £3,979 | £796 | £838 | £1,591 | £1,675 | 5.3% |
| Vauxhall Corsa 1.3 | D | £15,045 | 112 | 13% | £1,956 | £391 | £481 | £782 | £963 | 23.0% |
| Volvo C30 1.6 D2 ES | D | £17,940 | 114 | 13% | £2,332 | £466 | £574 | £933 | £1,148 | 23.0% |

Figures courtesy of www.comcar.co.uk

The examples given above are not necessarily representative of that particular type of car. There is such a wide range within each make/model that it is not possible to select one that is typical in terms of list price or $CO_2$ emissions. For further information you should visit the manufacturer's website or speak to their sales staff.

The last column shows the increase in the actual tax liability. As already mentioned earlier in this book, the general 1% uplift in the taxable percentages for each $CO_2$ band bears more heavily on cars with lower emissions as it causes the tax bill to increase by a greater proportion. You will see this if you compare the last column with the $CO_2$ column.

The tax bill on the Jaguar does not go up at all as it is already at the maximum 35%, as are all cars with $CO_2$ emissions above 225 g/km. The only other cars where the tax bill will not change in

April 2012 are those below 100 g/km (which still qualify for the 10% band) and between 121-124 g/km (which will remain at 15%).

However, the taxable percentages on cars with $CO_2$ emissions between 100-120 g/km are going up from 10% to 11-15% in April 2012, and this will cause tax bills on these cars to increase by up to 50% in one year. This is reflected in the figures for the Ford Mondeo, the Ford Ka, the Vauxhall Agila, the Vauxhall Corsa, the Nissan Micra, the Seat Altea and the Volvo C30.

## Notes for Employers

For employers, the main tax consideration is $CO_2$ emissions. These affect both capital allowances and lease rentals.

Cars with emissions in excess of 160 g/km should be avoided, as capital allowances for cars in this bracket are going down to 8% per annum from April 2012, whilst for leased cars 15% of the monthly rentals do not qualify for tax relief.

The $CO_2$ emissions also affect the Class IA national insurance employers have to pay on company cars. These are based on the taxable percentage for each car and, as we have already seen, these will be increasing significantly for some cars in April 2012.

Cars which may seem tax efficient at the moment will incur higher national insurance charges from 2012/13 onwards. If you want to keep down your PAYE bill, you need to choose company cars with care.

However, if you are planning to introduce a car club for your employees, linked to a salary sacrifice scheme, you may wish to recommend cars with lower $CO_2$ emissions as otherwise the scheme may not produce a tax saving and employees would be better off buying or leasing the car themselves.

It may even be a good idea to include a table in your scheme literature for employees, showing how much their take home pay will go down for different types of car.

# Conclusion

When I was asked by Taxcafe to write this book the original idea was that it would serve as mini-guide for people working through their own companies. The main issue I wanted to address was whether it was worth having a company car or not.

As the subject unfolded it became apparent that it was much broader in scope than first envisaged and that the book would appeal to a much wider group of people. Therefore, I decided to aim it at sole traders and employees too and address issues of particular interest to them, such as capital allowances, cash alternatives and salary sacrifice schemes.

Consequently this book is much longer than we first planned. I hope, however, that it has been a good read and helped you to understand the complicated world of tax in a new light in as much as it affects cars and vans. More importantly, I hope that it will prove to be of practical help to you in your own working life.

The first 7 chapters of this book look at the detailed tax rules and all the relevant factors you have to consider. It is a bit of a hard slog if you find the subject about as interesting as watching paint dry, but a working knowledge of how the tax system works will reap benefits when you get to the second part of the book, which is how to actually save tax.

The remaining 10 chapters each consider a different question – the sort of questions that would occur to anyone who uses a car in their work. Hopefully they will help to answer those questions.

The question on whether to have a company car for your own business is by far the longest chapter in the book. There are so many relevant factors impinging on this decision that the case studies have had to deal with quite a few variations in the facts presented.

As most accountants will tell you, the usual answer to this question is an emphatic No. The received wisdom is that it is better for you to run your own car and claim mileage instead. It is generally assumed that company car tax is so steep these days that it is not worth having one if you run your own business.

However, Chapter 8 identifies several scenarios where the opposite is true, and to be absolutely sure you really need to run your own figures through the templates.

If you are driving a low emissions car it may well be beneficial for you to put it through your company, especially if you are leasing it, as VAT registered businesses will typically save around £200 a year on the monthly rentals.

That is because you can recover 50% of the VAT on a leased car, whereas you cannot recover any VAT at all if you purchase a car that has any private use whatsoever. High maintenance bills are another factor in favour of company cars as they are tax deductible and you can also recover the VAT.

More surprisingly, high business mileage is a factor against company cars, as the approved tax-free mileage rates available to directors using their own cars are higher than the advisory fuel rates used by company car drivers, despite the fact that they were frozen at 40p per mile for 9 years.

Of course, the tax-free mileage rates also cover other running costs, including depreciation, so they are not directly comparable with the advisory fuel rates. Nonetheless, the case studies show that high business mileage tends to sway the decision against company cars.

It may also come as a surprise that higher-rate taxpayers who run their **own** businesses are better off with company cars than most basic-rate taxpayers, despite the fact that they pay double the amount of tax on them. That is because they would usually have to pay higher-rates of tax on an extra dividend instead if they chose to buy the car themselves. Also, the company can claim capital allowances whereas directors using their own cars cannot.

Company cars are also more tax efficient if your company pays high rates of corporation tax. This can push the breakeven $CO_2$ emissions level up to around 160 g/km, whereas for a company paying 20% tax it would normally be around 120-129 g/km. A company can claim all running costs against tax without any private use deduction, so the higher its tax rate the more it can save. In contrast, all an employee can claim against tax is the 45p mileage rate.

For sole traders and partnerships (or at least the ones with turnover below the VAT threshold) the most important question is whether to claim the tax free mileage rates or a proportion of capital allowances and running costs.

Chapter 9 explores this subject in some detail, and comes to the conclusion that running costs are generally more tax efficient than the mileage rates, perhaps not surprisingly given that they were frozen for so long.

Of course, the biggest running cost these days is fuel, and as fuel prices go up so the mileage rates become less attractive. They may be more advantageous for smaller cars with lower running costs, but your business mileage (or business use proportion) would need to be fairly low for the approved mileage rates to be the better option.

For employees, Chapters 14-17 are the most relevant part of the book, dealing with issues such as cash alternatives, salary sacrifice schemes and fuel cards.

Unsurprisingly, basic-rate taxpayers benefit more from their company cars than higher-rate taxpayers. They pay only half as much tax on them and also save more on employee national insurance contributions, which are not due on company cars and other such benefits.

Higher-rate taxpayers also save national insurance but for them the advantage is less because they would only have to pay 2% on the equivalent amount of salary, whereas a basic-rate taxpayer would pay 12%.

For higher-rate taxpayers, the saving between the tax they pay on their company cars and what it would cost them to run their own cars is much less than for a basic-rate taxpayer.

In fact, sometimes there is no financial advantage at all in a company car. A cash alternative is a much more viable option for higher-rate taxpayers as their employers do not need to offer them so much. True, they would have to pay higher rates of tax on a cash alternative instead, but overall they would only pay about one-third more tax and national insurance on a cash alternative than a basic-rate taxpayer (42% against 32%) whereas on a company car they would pay double (40% against 20%).

Apart from your marginal tax rate, the other major factor affecting the decision on whether to have a company car or a cash alternative is the Taxable Percentage. This is based mainly on $CO_2$ emissions (fuel type also plays a part as there is a 3% surcharge on diesels) and the lower the emissions the harder it is for the employer to make an economic offer.

That is because the employee saves tax on lower emissions but the employer does not really save much at all apart from the Class 1A national insurance charge. Therefore, at lower $CO_2$ levels, the saving the employer makes in not running a company car does not keep pace with the higher incremental cost for the employee in having to run his/her own car.

Other factors also play a part. Running costs can be a major factor. If an employee can save say 25% on the maintenance bills compared to his/her employer, it is much more likely that a cash alternative is viable.

Business mileage is also important. If you do a lot of business mileage in your company car, you are paying a lot of extra tax for perhaps relatively low private use. You might be better off running your own car and claiming mileage expenses, although you should bear in mind that the main 45p rate is unlikely to cover your average cost per mile.

As for fuel, we all know that prices at the pumps are going through the roof at the moment and there is no sign of them coming back down again. Chapter 16 examines whether fuel cards are worth it, or more exactly whether it is worth letting your employer pay for private fuel.

It has been a bit of an urban myth in recent years that private fuel is no longer worth it because of the high tax charges. Certainly the tax on private fuel paid by the employer has gone up a lot lately, but not anything like as much as fuel prices. In fact, basic-rate taxpayers are still usually better off with employer-paid private fuel if they do around 4,000 private miles a year. For higher-rate taxpayers it would need to be double.

However, the decision rests on many other factors, in particular the Taxable Percentage for your car. For cars with higher levels of $CO_2$ emissions it would be a lot more difficult to make private fuel pay as the benefit-in-kind could be anything up to 35% of £18,800. That is the absolute maximum however. Most cars would probably be no higher than 23%, which for 2011/12 equates to $CO_2$ emissions of 165-169 g/km for a petrol-fuelled car (or 150-154 g/km for a diesel). It also depends on the fuel consumption of your car and, most of all, the cost of fuel.

If you've made it all the way through this book, from cover to cover, many congratulations. If this book enables you to save as much tax on your car as some of my clients have done over the years, then it is both time and money well spent.

Lightning Source UK Ltd.
Milton Keynes UK
UKOW030904210512

192975UK00001B/9/P